INSTITUTE OF ECONOMICS
AND STATISTICS
OXFORD

P

KU-309-288

How to Use
Cost Benefit Analysis
in Project Appraisal

WITHDRAWN

ECONOMICS
LIBRARY
STATISTICS

WITHDRAWN

How to Use
Cost Benefit Analysis
in Project Appraisal

Michael J Frost

WITHDRAWN

9 MAR 1976

Gower Press

First edition published under the title of
Values for Money
by Gower Press Limited, Epping, Essex
1971

Second impression 1971

Second edition published under the title of
How to Use Cost Benefit Analysis in Project Appraisal
1975

© Michael J Frost 1971, 1975

ISBN 0 7161 0276 5

Set in 11/13 Press Roman
Printed in Great Britain by Biddles Ltd, Guildford, Surrey

Contents

v

Illustrations

Figure

Preface

Since writing the earlier version of this book, I have been working as a consultant in the public sector both in the UK and in a number of overseas countries. I have watched the Roskill Commission come and go, Maplin rise and fall and a new mood of self-questionning arise both within the UK Civil Service and in the ranks of many professions such as architects, planners and economists. A Minister in the last UK Conservative Government felt that the solution to our problems lay in the greater use of public opinion in deciding issues such as those raised in this book, and that analysis would therefore take a back seat.

Although many of these developments are discouraging, I have been heartened by the attitude of a number of leading planners and civil servants such as Wilfred Burns to whom thanks are due for producing the very positive foreword to this book. In this he recognizes that many public sector problems are too complex to be solved by preconceived formulae, and that some way must be found of taking into account the mass of quantitative and qualitative data now available. The main points which I have tried to bring out in this book, and in the studies for which I have been responsible are as follows.

1 The existence of alternatives; solutions rarely drop out of thin air even onto the drawing board of the most respected international experts.

2 Accepting that conventional constraints can be relaxed may open Pandora's box. The range of possibilities for dealing with most problems in public policy is amazingly large, and this calls for a realistic approach to short listing. It is ludicrous if all the resources available for a study are spent on the detailed evaluation of an arbitrarily chosen short list.

3 It is no longer good enough to look at problems of public policy from the narrow viewpoint of pure economics; techniques are available for assembling a great deal of data on their sociological and technical impact, and on the ways in which decisions taken now will interact with the future. However, many debates have degenerated into slanging matches between such groups as economists, environmentalists, planners, businessmen, and so on. Some way must be found of encouraging these people to discuss problems in a sensible way. My experience of the methods set out in this book is that they do just that.

Perhaps even more important than these factors is the question of public opinion; this varies considerably from one country to another. For example, in a recent French study on the alignment of a motorway, the consultants took the precaution of carrying out a limited public opinion survey. The vast majority of the replies were to the effect that such a complex problem could only be decided by suitably qualified experts, and that they had every confidence in them. In countries such as the UK, where the whole role of experts is far more strenuously challenged, it is vital to take an objective view of the way in which public opinion on such issues is formed. A very effective way of committing political suicide is to carry out a study without making a very serious effort to ensure that the main facts are presented to the public in an objective way; there are almost always plenty of people with a strong financial or other interest who will ensure that their voice is clearly heard. In this process of putting over a message to the public on socio-economic problems, three stages seem to me to be essential.

(a) To have a clear idea of what the public understands by certain basic terms such as profit, inflation, and so on. One of the reasons for the relatively high level of economic debate in France is that the Government has gone to some lengths to couch its arguments in terms which really are understood, and to conduct research to ensure that this is so. A striking example of the contrary situation was the way in which the argument over miners' pay and inflation was put forward to the British electorate in 1974.

(b) The argument must be conducted in an intelligible framework and must include representatives from at least the more serious media. Compared even to the standard of macro-economic debate, the treatment of micro-economic problems such as those set out in this book is bedevilled by the lack of agreement on such a framework. A particularly glaring example is the amazing diversity of attitudes to the notion of business profit.

(c)   Resources must be available for some form of public relations action to ensure that the main media and appropriate opinion formers understand the study which has been carried out.

Unfortunately, civil servants in many countries are most unwilling to provide the resources for public relations exercises of this kind. In particular much of the circular discussion on airport planning in the UK can be traced back to shortcomings in the way in which the original study was presented to politicians and the public.

Michael J Frost

Foreword

The amount of information available to decision makers now tends to be overwhelming. Yet knowledge increases year by year and, in relation to public projects, the necessity for more public participation extends still further the range of information that has to be considered. We no longer think in terms of a scheme or project but of alternative solutions to problems.

The techniques of evaluation have correspondingly improved. Indeed, the information explosion made the evaluation explosion inevitable. Means had to be found for marshalling data into useable and comparable form as far as possible so that those involved in decision making could make sense of the masses of information at their disposal.

It is necessary, I think, to approach evaluation in this way because it is then obvious that one is not simply concerned with the activities of one profession, nor is one constrained to attempt to put every effect into money or, indeed, measured terms. The object of evaluation is to reduce the number of variables as far as is sensible so that those who take decisions can more readily comprehend the effects, costs, benefits, values, and public acceptability.

Many professions will thus contribute to the evaluation process: ecologists as well as economists, architects, surveyors, engineers, planners and the physically based professions, as well as sociologists, political scientists and others with skills in a totally different field. Their contributions will vary; some may be able to contribute data in statistical or mathematical form, but some may contribute value assessments that cannot be so measured and classified. Everything relevant needs to be incorporated into the evaluation process.

Naturally all this is complicated and sometimes highly technical, but we will lose a great deal if we simply regard evaluation as one more technical exercise to help the bureaucrats.

We need, therefore, to structure the evaluation questions so that proper use is made of the evaluation techniques that are available, but also to make sure that those aspects that cannot be incorporated are recorded rather than dismissed as irrelevant.

As more and more citizens take part in the discussion of public developments, it becomes important to help them to understand the complexity of the problem. The loudest voice is not necessarily the most important and by no means necessarily the best informed. Evaluation techniques should be designed to help everyone understand better the issues that have to be settled.

Economists, by their training and way of thinking, have, perhaps, been foremost in trying to develop the numerate approach to evaluation. At times, in the past, perhaps too much was claimed for cost benefit analysis. Now, however, many others are involved in evaluation procedures and a variety of techniques are available. Cost effectiveness studies and environmental impact studies are just two of them. Cost benefit analysis itself has also been developed and the understanding of its role in decision making become better understood.

This book is a revised version of an earlier one by the author and itself shows how our understanding is being progressively improved. It is another contribution to this important developing field.

Wilfred Burns, CB, CBE, DSc, PPRTPI, MICE
Deputy Secretary and Chief Planner,
Department of Environment

Part One

Principles of
Cost Benefit Analysis

1

Quantifiable Methods in Decision Making

A FEW EXAMPLES

Cost benefit analysis is designed to compare two or more solutions to a given problem and to provide a framework in which such comparisons can be usefully discussed. Starting from a few clearly defined assumptions it relies on the preferences expressed by the members of the group concerned by the decision; in this sense, it is profoundly democratic. Many of these preferences concern normal economic goods and are revealed by the price mechanism; others involve factors such as noise and time for which there is no obvious market.

Before going any further it might be useful to look at the following examples.

1 Choices that are made by industrial firms and that are expressed almost entirely in traditional economic terms. Examples are the problems faced by a business when deciding whether: to adopt a new price for one of its goods, to install new plant or to build a factory in one location rather than another; these are usually a question of maximizing profit or yield on capital.

2 Choices that are made in the public interest but which are still concerned with traditional economic arguments. These may concern a local authority faced with the location of a new industrial area or the building of a bridge or motorway.

3 More complex problems which move outside the area of traditional economics and consider social factors such as the value of life and death, the

value of time, the distribution of income, etc. Here one might quote decisions made by local or central authorities on building a hospital to cut motor accident deaths, introducing a speed limit to reduce the accident rate itself, or the introduction of a new system of personal taxation.

OPPOSITION TO QUANTIFIED METHODS

Although there are notable exceptions, many such decisions are taken without attempting to introduce quantified techniques and it may be useful to look at some of the reasons why this is so.

In both industrial and public decision making there has been considerable opposition to quantified techniques. Those wishing to use such methods should be aware of the main arguments against them.

Failure to recognize alternatives

It often happens that decision makers just do not want to know about the possibility of an alternative. For example, a marketing manager, faced with a price reduction from one of his competitors, may state that it is inconceivable that he should not also reduce his prices. Although he might be willing to admit that maintaining the present level is a theoretical possibility, he may prefer not to consider this seriously but rely on his own established rule: 'We always follow our competitor'.

Similarly when discussing the construction of a new factory, rather than enlarging an existing one, a technical director may state flatly that it is 'obvious' that such an extension would be 'impossible'. In the field of public decision a similar unyielding position may be met with statements such as: 'We can't let this country's shipbuilding industry disappear'.

It is most important to appreciate that attitudes of this kind are often very deeply felt and that suggestions that the 'ridiculous' alternative may be a real one, are likely to be met with considerable scorn: 'It's obvious that you haven't been in this business very long'.

A very important point in dealing with such arguments is that few solutions are strictly impossible, and that the choice is almost always expressible in terms of cost. For example, in a factory the introduction of labour-saving machinery is sometimes only supported by the argument: 'If we don't, we shall never get the labour'. It is interesting to trace through the justification of such an attitude, by asking questions on the lines of: 'Supposing you needed extra men for an expansion programme how would you get them?' In one rather striking case, the answer was to organize a bus to a nearby town at a cost which represented only a few per cent of the basic wage rate.

Similarly in the field of public decision, a statement that it would be 'impossibly expensive' to place electricity transmission lines underground, is often seen in much better perspective if this cost is actually quantified; here it may turn out that in some circumstances society is prepared to pay the cost, in order to avoid damaging a particularly beautiful piece of landscape.

'Romantics'

The second objection to quantification comes from those who are resolutely against quantification. In its purest form this attitude is used by romantics, who allege that the use of quantified methods is likely to bring about a world of grey monotony — a kind of 1984. On a rather more everyday level, one has met with marketing directors who are prepared to accept the results of market research, as long as these confirm their own attitude; however, they would not be prepared to base their decisions on these quantified techniques alone.

This is sometimes due to a genuine mistrust of the technique, based on the thought that a manager has to deal with a wide range of decisions and that quantified methods cannot possibly keep pace with all of them. However, it also contains an element of: 'It is much more exciting to take decisions based on intuition (perhaps called experience or judgement), without being limited by having to justify them in rational terms'. Similar attitudes are also frequent in public administration, where it is felt that some matters are 'properly left to politicians', and that any attempt at quantification is an infringement on some sacred prerogative.

Faced with this second kind of objection the best tactic is to emphasize that quantified methods do not replace judgement; they provide a rational basis on which judgement can properly be exercised.

Methods not yet ripe

The third argument commonly used against quantification is that the methods available are not yet fully developed, or are incapable of taking into account all the various aspects of the problem. Unfortunately such feelings are only too justified in many cases and the following arguments are often useful.

1 'A decision has to be taken; if you are not prepared to use such quantified methods as are available (or could be reasonably easily developed) how do you propose to proceed?' Such an approach is often particularly useful when dealing with problems that are bound to come up fairly frequently, for example, pricing decisions within industry or planning problems in the public sector. The development of suitable methods and measurement techniques is sometimes a fairly costly business, and someone has often to put forward the resources to develop them to the stage at which they make a genuine contribution.

2 'What are the factors that, in your opinion, have been left out?' In a marketing situation traditional price/volume analysis may ignore the effect of sales of one product on those of the rest of the company's range. A marketing man may say: 'Although an investment in X is not profitable in its own right, think of the effect on the other products'.

The identification of such additional considerations may be a fairly big step in the direction of taking them into account; it may be fairly easy to see whether, on any reasonable assumption, the effect in question is likely to be material. An example in the public sector might be the discussion of a decrease in parking fines so as to encourage people to pay them and thereby maximize income for the local authority; an objection might be that this has a discouraging effect on the general law-abidingness of the population. Having identified this item it might well be possible to go on and quantify it, or at least obtain an idea of whether it could outweigh all the other strictly economic considerations.

BUSINESS DECISIONS : DISCOUNTED CASH FLOW

Most businessmen are now familiar with quantified methods designed to help them in their decisions. One of the most satisfactory and comprehensive of these is to forecast the implications of a decision and to compare the two alternatives by means of a discounted cash flow.

The following table (Table 1.1) is a simple example of this. This gives the cash generated by a business investment: it is discounted at various rates of interest to find the 'yield' at which the present volume of all the inflows (benefits) equals the present value of all the outflows (costs). In the example the yield is 16 per cent as the total of the figures in the last line is approximately zero.

Where this quantified approach has failed to play a real part in the taking of decisions this is generally because of the following causes.

1 Those responsible for the decision have not been willing to clarify their assumptions and in particular have passed the whole job on to the long-suffering accountant. The only person capable of making assumptions about the elasticity of demand is the marketing manager.

2 Lack of imagination in applying the method and in particular failure to take into account points which are vital to those making the decision, but which do not fit into the existing accounting framework. Such attitudes are not uncommon even among competent management accountants, and can be rendered still more damaging if the decision maker is unconvinced by the whole accounting treatment of some transaction. An example of this latter point often concerns the interminable argument over the allocation of overhead expenses.

3 The analysis has not begun early enough in the process to have any real effect. It is vital to start sketching out rough estimates before ideas have become fixed.

Cash Flow (£'000)

	Initial Outlay	1	2	3	4	5	6	7	8	9	10
Fixed assets											
Plant	120	120	120	120	120	150	150	150	150	150	—
Buildings	84	84	84	84	84	84	84	84	84	84	—
Depreciation											
Plant	—	(12)	(24)	(36)	(48)	(60)	(78)	(96)	(114)	(132)	—
Buildings	—	(1)	(2)	(3)	(4)	(5)	(6)	(7)	(8)	(9)	—
Net fixed assets	204	191	178	165	152	169	150	131	112	93	—
Working capital	70	70	140	182	280	280	280	280	280	280	—
Total net assets	274	261	318	347	432	449	430	441	392	373	—
Movement in net assets	(274)	13	(57)	(29)	(85)	(17)	19	19	19	19	373
Profit before tax	—	7	40	65	121	135	135	135	135	135	135
Taxes payable	—		(3)	(16)	(26)	(48)	(54)	(54)	(54)	(54)	(108)
Cash flow	(274)	20	(20)	20	10	70	100	100	100	100	400
Discount rate (16%)	1.000	0.8621	0.7432	0.6407	0.5523	0.4761	0.4104	0.3538	0.3050	0.2630	0.2267
Present value at 16%	(274)	17	(15)	13	11	33	41	35	31	26	91

TABLE 1.1

THE APPROPRIATE METHOD

Most decisions can be divided into three main stages.

1 The generation and initial retention of ideas.
2 A short listing procedure.
3 The final analysis of a small number of schemes.

The detailed application of cost benefit analysis as described in this book, is normally only applicable to the last of these stages. It would often be excessively expensive to apply it to the large number of solutions that could be conceivably adopted.

The problem of short listing is to balance the resources used to carry out the process against the decision-makers confidence in the final result. In a great many studies the temptation to move to the apparent security of detailed calculation is overwhelming and as a result perfectly good solutions are rejected at an early stage. A particularly dangerous method of carrying out such a short listing is to apply a series of criteria individually in the form of 'acceptable solutions'. For example, in the case of a motorway, there might be an upper limit to the cost per mile, a lower limit to the distance between the motorway and a village of a certain size, and so on. Even if such a procedure is feasible in that it leaves solutions which obey all the rules, it is likely to lead to the selection of ideas that offend nobody. In particular it will not explore the relative importance of the different criteria.

A number of methods have been developed to deal with this kind of problem. They are sometimes referred to as the multiple criteria approach, and a fairly extensive body of literature is now available on them. This is described in more detail in Chapter 3.

PUBLIC DECISION : COST BENEFIT ANALYSIS

The discounted cash flow method considers only very small segments of the economy and in particular the effects of the decision on an individual firm. It is not concerned with two important external effects.

1 The effect of the decision on other people: for example, a given price increase may well be beneficial to the company making it, but will undoubtedly make life harder for the consumer. Similarly the decision to build a new factory may have economic effects on a whole range of suppliers and on the local economy. Businessmen are, however, increasingly having to take into account such effects on third parties. A particularly striking example is the need to look at the effect on the local economy when proposing to set up a company in an underdeveloped country (*see* Chapter 11, page 135).

2 The effect on what is loosely termed the environment. Even quite normal business decisions are likely to have effects on such factors as noise, pollution, visual amenity, and so on, and it is likely that businessmen will have to take these into account more and more. If they do not, they will be met with apparently arbitrary restrictions, which could sometimes have been avoided if the situation had been analysed from the community's point of view in the first place.

A resource which is often left out of business calculations is time. An example might concern the location of a factory; the time spent by workers getting to and from their homes is likely to be evaluated by them and expressed either in terms of claims for shorter working hours or additional remuneration to offset the loss of leisure time.

In purely public decisions all these socio-economic factors are likely to be of even greater importance, as are others such as the valuation of human life, the value of education, or the asset represented by a law-abiding population.

Cost benefit analysis is an extension of the techniques used for individual business decisions (and in particular discounted cash flow), and is designed to cover these two omissions. Thus it deals with all firms and individuals in a community and also both economic and socio-economic terms. To illustrate this the following example may be useful (Table 1.2).

	Operators	Other travellers	General public	Total
	(£'000)	(£'000)	(£'000)	(£'000)
Loss to operators	−50			−50
Loss of time to other travellers		−20		−20
Noise			+20	+20
Reduction in traffic accidents	+10	+40	+20	+70
Fines collected	−5		+ 5	
Cost of control				−10
Total	−45	+20	+35	+10

Table 1.2

This shows the effects of a proposal to impose a speed limit on heavy vehicles on a stretch of urban road. It shows some of the losses and gains in the overall evaluation and also the incidence of these effects on various members of the community.

Viewed from the operator's point of view, this project would cause a loss of £45 000; the reduction in traffic accidents is more than outweighed by the loss of time and the cost of fines that will be paid. However, there is a gain to other travellers and more particularly to the general public. Looked at in another way the effects of time and noise on the general public cancel out, and the gain due to a lower accident rate more than outweighs the loss to goods operators and the cost of administering the system.

IDENTIFICATION OF CHOICE

In the same way as for decisions taken by individual businesses, the starting point is to identify the choice that is to be made. In particular, if some line of action is being vigorously proposed, it is vital that the alternative should be clearly stated and explored. In an industrial context the reaction of a marketing manager faced with undercapacity in a factory, may well be to say that it would be unthinkable not to invest in new plant. However, it is essential that he should be made to admit that some solution could be envisaged if capacity were not available, for example, raising prices so as to damp down demand.

Similarly in the field of public investment the alternative must be faced even if this has extremely unpleasant consequences. A striking example is in the field of public health; the alternative to building a hospital is to accept a lower standard of health, and even death in some cases, for the population at large. Here those responsible may be most unwilling to envisage this outcome and may attempt to take refuge behind 'such a solution would be unthinkable'.

It is sometimes useful to distinguish between two cases.

1 Those in which there are a limited number of fairly clearly defined alternatives. The rest of this book will be essentially discussing situations in which the choice has been boiled down to two. Those in which there are a finite number of fairly clearly defined alternatives. The normal procedure here is to apply some form of short listing procedure and then to analyse the small number of projects in detail. Short listing methods are discussed in Chapter 3 and most of the rest of this book is concerned with the final stage of detailed analysis.

2 The more general case, in which there is an infinite range of possible solutions. Sometimes we are able to apply optimizing techniques such as linear programming to these; examples might be the determination of the optimum size of ships, the best date for carrying out some investment or the best network of depots to ensure distribution of a product. If such optimization is not possible it is necessary to draw up a long list of solutions which adequately represents the range.

When defining alternatives it is most important to see that each solution is sub-optimized, that is, that it represents the most efficient arrangement possible for that alternative. For example, if we are considering the construction of a motor-way, it is essential that this should be the most economic, technical solution possible and equally that the alternative with which we are comparing it, for example, the improvement of existing roads, should also be the most economic in its field.

To go back to our marketing example involving undercapacity, the marketing manager may well say that it would be unthinkable to limit capacity to present levels; this would lead to an out-of-stock situation which would gravely harm the company's marketing image. In fact it would very soon become apparent that such a situation would never be allowed to develop, and that the true alternative would involve some method of damping down demand.

Often by pursuing this question whether the alternative is the best possible, it becomes apparent that the problem is not to choose whether to do something or not, but rather one of timing (*see* the example in Chapter 5, page 55).

DECIDING WHAT FORECASTS NEED TO BE MADE

The first problem to be faced in forecasting the implications of any choice, is that of deciding what to forecast. This is where one sees the value of a comprehensive theoretical framework capable of answering questions such as those following.

1 Should we analyse a situation before or after tax; in the case of the latter is it necessary to look at the uses to which taxation is put?

2 Supposing we are considering the profit of an industry; is it necessary to know what will happen to this by way of dividends, retained profits, and so on?

3 Many economic decisions involve a whole chain of suppliers. How far back along this chain do we have to go?

4 Should we take into account the effect of price changes?

5 Should all the transactions be measured at current market prices or is some kind of adjustment required? Is it necessary to forecast such price changes?

The kind of treatment described in Chapter 2 gives the answers to most of these questions. In many other cases it is possible to see whether detailed forecasts are required, by an assessment of the order of magnitude of any likely difference. There is obviously no point in forecasting something that cannot conceivably affect the outcome.

TECHNIQUES OF FORECASTING

Cost benefit analysis is concerned with evaluating the future; the validity of its results, therefore, depends absolutely upon the value of the forecasting methods used. These are discussed in Chapter 3. Sometimes it is possible to express such estimates as a rudimentary kind of probability distribution; even when this is not so, it is most important that the economist should attempt to estimate the degree of reliability that can be put on any individual forecast. These estimates form the starting point for the sensitivity analysis that is described later in this chapter.

EVALUATION OF FORECASTS

Having made forecasts of the physical consequences of the various alternatives these must be related in some way. There are three main schools of thought as to how this can be done.

1 The various terms should be made directly comparable by expressing them in a common unit, usually money. This is the ideal method, as it provides a much better framework for discussion and consideration of the individual terms and it is the one we shall adopt in this book.

2 Some people feel that a great many important factors in a major decision can not possibly be quantified; they consider that the decision should be arrived at by a more or less subjective weighting together of a large number of different measures, some of which are quantified and others not.

3 A third approach, which is somewhere between the first two, accepts that in principle it would be better if all the aspects of the forecasts could be expressed in money terms, but that in practice this is often impossible. In order to meet this problem they have devised a number of multi-criteria methods such as those described in Chapter 3 (*see* page 31).

One rather special objection to expressing the whole range of human activity in money terms should perhaps be mentioned. This is that there is something degrading about valuing, say, human health in terms of money that might have been spent on bingo. This ignores the fact that the same money could well have been spent on a health programme, and that in determining the size of such a programme this kind of quantification is more or less inevitable. We are not trying to say that money is the most important factor in our lives but simply that it is a convenient way in which to express other factors such as comfort, the satisfaction obtained by various forms of consumption or the enjoyment of a quiet afternoon in the garden.

This in no way confirms the preponderance of money in public decision; the whole object of cost benefit analysis is to place the value of living in a pollution-free environment in the same balance as a company's profits. The latter have often decided issues in the past; the aim of a wider form of analysis is to ensure that they do not do so at the expense of environmental factors which have often remained unquantified.

The quantification of traditional economic terms is fairly well understood. The main theoretical question on which our analytical framework must provide guidance is that if price changes; in particular we must distinguish between two extreme cases.

1 A manufacturer's price change, which does not necessarily reflect any change in the value of the commodity, but which merely transfers costs from the manufacturer to the consumer.

    Consider a rise in the price of cigarettes; in the case considered this was designed to bring the manufacturer extra revenue and did not relate to any change in the product. The consumer experiences a certain pleasure as the result of smoking a cigarette and it seems reasonable to state that within limits this does not depend upon the price. For example, an air traveller who buys a carton of cigarettes at half price does not enjoy them any more or less because of this.

    It is of course true that as a result of the price rise he is forced by the income constraint to spend less on some items of consumption, including perhaps cigarettes. It is in this way that the price increase costs him something. It has no effect on the satisfaction obtained from a given cigarette and in particular it does not increase it.

2 A real effect such as the reduction in the cost of a journey resulting from the construction of a bypass.

The approach in Chapter 2 shows that for marginal economic changes the analysis should be carried out in constant prices as between the solutions compared.

More difficult problems are encountered in the quantification of items for which there is no market price, such as, time, noise, etc. These are dealt with in some detail in Chapter 5.

ASSEMBLY OF FORECASTS IN A LOGICAL FRAMEWORK

Cost benefit analysis is concerned with collecting a large number of terms, which represent the effect of the decision on different parts of society. There is clearly a possibility of double counting, or forgetting an item altogether. Furthermore, one may well devote considerable time and trouble to forecasting one item (for example, the costs of a particular company) only to find that it is automatically cancelled out by another item (its receipts) in a large number of cases. Equally, in economic discussion one often finds that two apparently conflicting statements may each be true within a given frame of reference, but that they are nevertheless incompatible.

For example, the aim of economic policy is sometimes said to be to increase wealth, that is, to maximize productive investments over a period. However, our approach, set out in Chapter 2, states that the primary objective is to increase consumption. For a given period these two statements are to some extent in conflict as it is possible to switch resources out of investment and into consumption. However, these concepts can be reconciled if we recognize that the object of wealth is to permit future consumption; thus, if we are carrying out an analysis over say ten years, the aim is to maximize a function of consumption during the period and wealth at the end of it. In order to compare these two factors we could express the wealth in terms of the future benefits that it will make possible.

The reason for such difficulties as these is that there is no generally accepted framework for discussion. For example, in the discussions of the Roskill Commission* the Research Team had worked within a framework in which the idea of company profit was absent. As will be seen from Chapter 2 this notion is central to our particular presentation.

AFFECTED PARTIES

The whole point of cost benefit analysis is that it takes into account the effects on a large number of parties. In the example given earlier in this chapter, the introduction of a speed limit will impose costs on public transport operators but benefits both for other motorists and for the public at large. Questions that this raises are as follows.

1 Can we simply add up the effects on the different parties expressed in money terms, or must we apply some form of weighting factor? For example consider the choice between taking 20 metres off a poor man's garden or the same 20 metres off a rich man's park; if the market value of these two pieces of land were equal, could society be said to be indifferent to the solution ? This boils down to asking whether the community attaches as much importance to the rich man's £100 as to that of the poor man. This problem is discussed in Chapter 7.

2 What is the effect of compensation. Will the problem that we have just mentioned look different if compensation is paid to the two parties? This is also discussed in Chapter 7.

---

* The Roskill Commission was set up by the UK Government in 1968 to examine the siting of the Third London Airport; it used a Research Team which included Economists, Scientists, Traffic Experts and Engineers, who conducted the cost benefit analysis.

SENSITIVITY ANALYSIS AND JUDGEMENT

Some of the criticisms levelled at cost benefit analysis have been that it eliminates the use of judgement. However, any analysis is based upon a list of assumptions which may arise either in forecasting, in quantification or as a result of theoretical considerations. Deciding which of these assumptions are correct and the direction and extent of likely errors is, however, essentially a matter of judgement. For example, if a decision on the building of an urban motorway is dominated by the cost of noise, the decision maker must clearly exercize his judgement on whether the valuation finally decided upon is reasonable, whether the evidence produced to support it is scientifically respectable, and so on.

It was noted that a theoretical framework would give a guidance on the terms to be included; however, this still leaves room for a good deal of judgement and here again the decision-maker may well insist that additional terms be studied.

To take an example out of the area of traditional marketing; suppose that a product manager wishes to launch a new pack. The fact that he has quantified all his assumptions, and used the skill of a management accountant to demonstrate that such a launch would be profitable, does not detract from the judgement needed by the marketing director in deciding whether to go ahead or not. All the assumptions concerning sales levels, etc, are clearly open to be criticized – and very often are.

A useful way of aiding judgement is to make sure that the calculation includes sensitivity analysis. This means that some of the crucial assumptions should be selected and the result recalculated using different values. Thus in the marketing context one might say: 'That's all very well, but what happens if sales were only half your forecast level?'. Similarly in the case of the motorway, it would be interesting to see what would happen if noise values were assumed at half the level indicated by the best estimate. One might also look at the result of cars having higher than forecast noise output, or of the overall level of traffic being different from that initially estimated.

PRESENTATION

It is not sufficient to carry out valid analysis; the result must be well presented if the right decisions are to be taken. This involves not only the questions of layout of the analysis discussed in Chapter 8 but also the implications of public opinion.

The rejection of the conclusions of the Roskill Commission appears to have been due to the political unpopularity of its findings; this crucial point is discussed at some length in Chapter 12. The conclusions underline the vital role of good public relations; if a decision is to be left to public opinion it is fundamental that this opinion should be well and properly informed.

1 A brief description of the alternatives considered and the reasons why they were selected.

2 A summary of the results of the analysis.

3 A list of the principal assumptions upon which this is based.

4 The results of varying the crucial assumptions – sensitivity analysis.

SUMMARY

In spite of opposition from various sources, quantified methods are fairly widely accepted in industry for purely economic decisions. The extension of such methods to public decisions involving a large number of people and covering not only economic items but also things such as noise and time obviously poses many problems of forecasting and evaluation. In order to solve these one needs to develop a satisfactory theory. However, this should not be regarded as a machine for decisions but rather as an aid to judgement; at many points both in the theoretical development and in any particular application one will need to make assumptions that are all open to discussion and which can be profitably studied by sensitivity analysis.

The aim is to derive a method which will cover all the factors of a decision. We will try to avoid an end result in which economic terms have to be weighed against environmental factors without being able to give the decision maker any guidance as to exactly how this should be done.

2

Theoretical Principles

NEED FOR A THEORY

A sound theoretical background is required, not only to convince oneself that the analysis carried out is correct, but also to be able to explain it to other people. This latter point is particularly important when dealing with public decisions that have to obtain political acceptance; it is, nevertheless, also present within companies, for example, so that the reasons for overruling a subordinate decision may be clearly understood. Such a theoretical basis should have the following specific advantages.

1 In order to arrive at a method of calculation of reasonable dimensions, it will be necessary to make a number of assumptions. These may or may not be the subject of discussion; in any case it is vital that they should be clearly stated so that interested parties can be given an opportunity to challenge them. Furthermore, in any complicated problem the person carrying out the analysis is bound to have moments of doubt; the only way in which these can be resolved is by referring back to a clearly stated analytical framework.

For example, consider a statement: 'Transfer payments within the economy should be ignored'. In the case of tax this idea is usually based upon one of two assumptions about the way in which the Government behaves. If it works on a fixed budget, any movement in taxation arising out of an individual investment is adjusted somewhere else in the system. Alternatively it may vary its expenditure. In the latter event it is clear that the change in taxation can be ignored only if at the margin the Government obtains full value for its money. Thus the statement about transfer payments is not an absolute truth but the consequences of assumption is that in some circumstances could be challengeable.

2 It will avoid double counting or the omission of significant items.

3 It will encourage discussion. Unless the reasoning adopted is set out in some clear logical way there is always the likelihood that those concerned will find themselves arguing at cross purposes, as in the tax example we have just mentioned.

PUBLIC DECISIONS

Arrow[0] has stated that the only way in which a country can take consistent decisions is to behave as if they were an individual. The problem of political choice is discussed in Chapter 7. The discussion in this chapter looks at the methods that such an individual might reasonably apply when arriving at his choices; it is however, perhaps not unduly optimistic to hope that a large proportion of properly educated people would normally agree with his conclusions once they had been explained to them.

For example, in the case of the Third London Airport the final problem was to choose between four short listed sites. It was possible to find individuals prepared to classify these sites in any of the 24 possible orders. This was because they had made estimates in their own minds of the importance of the various criteria, and so on. Their choice would be affected by whether or not they have lived near one of the sites, or knew someone who did. However, as a result of the hearings of the Roskill Commission[1] there was a considerable narrowing of the field of choice, even among those representing conflicting interests, once the facts of the situation and their influence upon the analysis had been explained.

IN WHOSE INTEREST IS ONE DECIDING?

The starting point of any theoretical analysis must be the definition of the criterion that one is trying to maximize. This may be the good of an individual, of a firm, of a town, region or country. The interests of these various groups are often in conflict and a major step forward in the discussion has often been made once this is realized. However, it clearly means that the decision is likely to be different according to the community in question and, therefore, this must be clearly defined at the outset.

For example, some of the towns in South Wales have recently been worried by the drift of young people to Bristol, and proposals have been put forward for the building of a large entertainment centre in Swansea. Looked at from the point of view of an individual town it may well be possible to justify such an investment, whereas taking the region as a whole, and taking into account Bristol's losses, the project might be seen to be bad. Similarly, if a factory decides to economize on plant for treating effluent, this may well appear as a good thing in that company's accounts but bad from the point of view of the local community.

One of the objects of public policy should be to ensure that in such cases the interests of the various communities involved are made to coincide. This is particularly important when discussing compensation in Chapter 7, and is further analysed in Chapter 14.

WELFARE: COLLECTIVE UTILITY

For the development of a theory of collective utility there is much to be said for the use of a mathematical notation. However, the remainder of this chapter is written in purely descriptive terms. An outline of the mathematical theory is given in Appendix 1; the two are in a sense alternatives.

Any community is made up of individuals and the consideration of utility must, therefore, start with a look at the way in which an individual reacts to economic change. To do this we need to introduce the notion of satisfaction; this is the individual's subjective reaction to an economic state. (By economic state we mean a set of values of all the factors in the economy; this may cover a succession of periods in time.)

Following everyday language, we would say that the individual prefers the situation in which his satisfaction is greatest. It seems reasonable to state that on average an individual's satisfaction will be determined by his consumption of goods and services; however, these must be defined widely enough to include not only things for which there is an economic market, but also such socio-economic factors as the quality of his environment, for example, the absence of intrusive noise.

Furthermore, we must be in a situation in which the individual is able to choose his consumption: a normal free economy. As we will see later, some problems involve consumption that is forced on the consumer (for example, the moving costs of someone who is evicted) and which give him no satisfaction. Here a rather more detailed treatment is required (*see* page 22).

The following are everyday examples of this notion of consumption.

1 The man who wins a motor car in a raffle; he is pleased.

2 The family whose house is made quieter and less dangeroud because the street in front of it ceases to be used as a major thoroughfare.

3 The people in a region who benefit from the introduction of a public electricity supply.

4 The people in a nation who benefit from the security provided by a better system of armed forces.

It is clear that even at this stage we are touching on some fairly complex psychological problems. One often hears statements on the lines of: 'He is no happier
than he was when he had nothing'. Nevertheless, averaging over groups of people,
so as to ignore freak individual reactions, it seems reasonable to state that people's
satisfaction increases with their consumption of goods and services. It is perhaps
worth noting that people generally behave as if this were so; they use their money
to obtain such goods and services rather than, say, burning it.

A further assumption that we will now make, is that the utility of a community
is a function of the satisfaction of its members. As we have noted, these individual
satisfactions are not necessarily related to items concerning purely personal satisfaction, but may also cover communal advantages such as the defence of the state.
Further examples that are sometimes quoted are the attitude of a state towards
the total consumption of alcohol or the use of drugs. However, in a democratic
society these can normally be expressed in terms of the attitudes of members of
the community to these problems.

ECONOMIC CHANGE

The essence of our problem is to compare two possible economic states resulting
from a choice. First of all let us consider a marginal change affecting only one
period in time — say one year.

Suppose that this enables a certain group of individuals to increase their consumption of, for example, electricity without any offsetting affect on any other
consumption; such an offset would normally come as a result of their revenue
constraint. The satisfaction of these individuals will now increase, and in
Appendix 1 we come to the not surprising result that the value to them of this
increase is proportional to the quantity of the electricity consumed multiplied by
its price.

The use of price as a measure should not be unexpected if we make the
assumption that individuals arrange their consumption so as to maximize satisfaction, while respecting the constraint imposed by their income. This means that
at the margin the satisfaction obtained by the consumption of an additional unit
of any commodity will be proportional to its price. This can perhaps best be
illustrated by Table 2.1.

	Price £/unit	Marginal satisfaction/unit	Satisfaction/£
Housing	10	100	10
Food	2	30	15
Entertainment	12	60	5
Holidays	15	150	10

Table 2.1

If the situation in Table 2.1 were true, the individual concerned would be able to obtain 15 units of satisfaction by spending £1 extra on food, whereas he would only lose five units of satisfaction by saving £1 on entertainment. This means that he had not succeeded in optimizing his satisfaction. A little thought shows that such possibilities of improvement must always exist if marginal satisfaction is not proportional to price; thus it follows that, if satisfaction has been maximized, this proportionality must always exist.

The above argument is sometimes criticized on the grounds that people do not behave rationally and that prices are not, therefore, a satisfactory measure. Whilst this may be true for individuals taken in isolation, it seems reasonable to suppose that 'errors' in personal behaviour will cancel out; thus, taken over a reasonably large number of individuals, it can be said that price is a measure of marginal satisfaction.

At this point it is convenient to make the assumption that all consumers pay the same price for a given article or service − that there is a single price system. However, this assumption, which simplifies our calculation, is not vital to the theory.

CONSTANT PRICES

We have seen that with the exception of changes forced on him, the satisfaction of an individual depends upon his consumption of goods and services, providing these are defined widely enough and are not limited to traditional economic items. Furthermore, the satisfaction produced by a change in the consumption of any good is proportional to its existing price.

Thus the total change in satisfaction is proportional to the change in consumption of the various goods and services freely chosen by the consumer multiplied by their prices. It should be noted that it is not necessary to take into account any movements in prices providing it can be assumed that the quantities of any particular commodity consumed by an individual do not influence its price − no single individual has any material effect on the market.

This conclusion is not surprising, as can be seen by considering a simple example. Suppose that part of an individual's satisfaction is obtained by having a certain number of meals in a restaurant. If the restaurant puts up its prices, this will not make the meal any more or less attractive. Thus it can be said that the price change has no direct influence on this satisfaction. It is not the cost of the food or service which counts, but the amount of it which is consumed.

If the individual were able to influence the price by the quantity he buys, for example, by some form of volume discount, the price to be taken into account as a measurement of his marginal satisfaction would not be the overall price but that effective at the margin. For example, suppose that he were able to obtain a 5 per cent cut in price for every 10 per cent increase in consumption, this would mean that the effective marginal price would be only about half of the apparent one. However, in most problems such arrangements are not met with on any material scale.

COLLECTIVE UTILITY

We must now look at the way in which the collective utility is affected by a change in an individual's satisfaction; here the assumption about the optimal distribution of income has to be introduced (this is discussed in Chapter 7). This states that the community has no preference between giving an additional £1 to one individual rather than to another. If such an assumption is accepted, it is fairly obvious that the change in collective utility is equal to the sum of the changes in individual consumption, evaluated at the prices in force before the change is made.

HOW COLLECTIVE UTILITY IS MEASURED

Under a certain number of assumptions we have shown that the change in collective utility corresponding to an economic choice is equal to the change in consumption of all economic and socio-economic goods measured at the prices in force before the change takes place. These assumptions were as follows.

1 Collective utility is a function of the satisfactions of the members of the community.

2 That the satisfaction of individuals is a function of their consumption of goods and services.

3 That the individuals maximize their satisfaction.

4 That no single individual is able to influence the price structure by his actions.

5 That there exists a single price structure for all individuals.

6 That the distribution of income is optimal.

We now have to face the problem of measuring this expression. It would be a hopeless task to attempt to trace the effects of any economic change through to the final variation in consumption of consumer goods. For example, suppose we are considering the siting of a steelworks; as a result of our choice, the incomes and consumption of the people working in various industries could be changed as may be the quantity of steel produced and the price at which it is sold. The latter will influence the prices and quantities of steel products and thus those of all goods using steel products.

A way out of this difficulty is found by noting that the total of the changes in profit of all enterprises in the economy, measured at constant prices, is equal to the changes in consumption of all economic goods and services by individuals, also measured at constant prices, plus any change in the use of outside resources. This is because all changes in transactions between enterprises cancel out in the addition process and we are left with only the two ends of the chain: outside resources and the consumption of individuals. In this statement we should note the following points.

(a) The word 'enterprise' has been used to indicate that we are dealing not only with traditional companies, but also with any other body having an economic role, for example, a county council or the Government.

(b) 'Outside resources' refers to things like unemployment or imports, which may vary as a result of the economic choice.

(c) A rather special form of enterprise is the Government in its role as a tax collector; tax is discussed later in this chapter.

(d) By 'profit' is meant the difference between goods bought and goods sold — the cash flow of the business concerned. Thus an increase in stock will show up as a loss, as will any investment at the moment at which it takes place.

It may be useful to illustrate these notions by a simple example (Table 2.2) in which all transactions are at constant prices.

This example is concerned with a food manufacturer who has an extremely labour intensive product. He is trying to decide whether to change his product line and manufacturing methods so as to be more profitable. It is assumed that this decision is being taken from the point of view of the community. In particular the calculation of profit is based upon the same prices in both cases: (A) the present situation and (B) the new methods and product line. The decision will have an effect on manufacturers of food plant and on the public, both as a supplier of labour and as a consumer. The following points should be noted.

(i) As a result of the change, consumption of food products increases by 600 and that of other consumer products by 200. The total amount of labour used is unaffected and we would, therefore, say that collective utility had gone up by 800. The profit of the various companies involved has also gone up by 800 and this is the equality that we were out to prove.

(ii) It is assumed that the labour released by the operation (700 by the food manufacturer less 50 by the plant manufacturer) is absorbed by other companies. If this were not so, there could be a change in unemployment and this would be added back to the calculation (outside resources) as it would not constitute any real saving to the community.

(iii) A number of other industrial products are also affected, with the various companies concerned adjusting their production so as to maintain equality between supply and demand.

(iv) The profit of the column 'other companies' is assumed to be zero in both cases. This is an example of the assumption of optimum management of companies and it will be referred to again in the following section.

	Plant manufacturer (£'000)		Food manufacturer (£'000)		Farmer (£'000)		Other companies (£'000)		Individual consumption (£'000)	
	A	B	A	B	A	B	A	B	A	B
Labour	(150)	(200)	(1000)	(300)	(1200)	(1200	(4350)	(5000)	(6700)	(6700)
Steel	(450)	(400)	–	–	–	–	450	400	–	–
Food plant	100	800	(100)	(800)	–	–	–	–	–	–
Other plant	500	–	–	–	–	–	(500)	–	–	–
Food										
Raw material	–	–	(2000)	(2000)	2000	2000	–	–	–	–
Finished product	–	–	3000	3600	–	–	–	–	3000	3600
Other products										
Consumer	–	–	–	–	–	–	3900	4100	3900	4100
Industrial	–	–	–	–	(500)	(500)	500	500	–	–
Profit	–	200	(100)	500	300	300	–	–	200	1000

TABLE 2.2

As has just been shown, the expression for collective utility in terms of consumption can be rewritten as: the change in profit of all enterprises at constant prices, plus the change in utilization of outside resources, plus the effect on non-economic terms which do not enter into the books of any enterprise. To pursue the last example, suppose that the more mechanized form of production produces a great deal of noise, and that this makes life more difficult for people living around the factory. In this case we would have to subtract (from the increase in overall profit of 800) an amount to represent this nuisance.

OPTIMAL MANAGEMENT

The expression that we have just arrived at in terms of companies can be very considerably simplified by the assumption of the optimal management of business. The idea is that businesses so arrange their affairs that any marginal change would bring no variation in profit. For example, it is assumed that if extra sales are obtained, the cost of these, including the investment that they require, will be exactly equal to the additional revenue.

This notion enables us to state that for a large number of businesses in any marginal economic change the movement in profits is zero. It should be noted, however, that this does not imply that the effect on them is negligible, but simply that they have so optimized their economy that the changes in sales, and so on, do not affect their profit.

It may be useful to look at this situation in terms of geometry; the position is rather as if the company has been able to place itself on top of a fairly smoothly-shaped dome on which height 'represents' profit. It is unlikely that relatively small movements in any direction will have a material effect on this profit.

Once again, while it is unlikely that this rather idealized situation is true for any single firm it is a fair approximation for an industry taken as a whole.

A point that should be noted is that any such optimization is likely to take place after tax, as this is seen by companies as being a normal cost. When dealing with taxes based on profit the difference between a before-tax and an after-tax optimization is probably not all that great; however, if some taxes, such as purchase tax, are borne by a company, a calculation will need to be made of the increase or decrease in such tax. An example is given on page 135 and the relationship between a firm's interests and the public good is discussed in Chapter 14.

CONSUMPTION THAT PRODUCES NO SATISFACTION

Up to now we have assumed that any increase in consumption will produce an improvement in satisfaction that is proportional to the price of the article concerned multiplied by the change in quantity consumed. There is, however, one important exception to this which may be illustrated by the construction of a bypass round a city. One of the objects of this may be to reduce the loss of petrol due to transport users having to stand in long queues. It is clear, however, that the reduction in consumption of petrol does *not* produce any reduction in the satisfaction of the people concerned. This is because the goods and services with which they are concerned are not the consumption of petrol but the accomplishment of a certain journey.

As a result of building the bypass, this journey can be carried out with less consumption of petrol; however, satisfaction remains the same and travellers have gained the petrol that would otherwise have been consumed. Terms of this kind must, therefore, be corrected for and this means adding to our expression for collective utility the sum of any changes in consumption that do not produce any additional satisfaction.

MARGINAL AND STRUCTURAL CHANGES

Our argument has been expressed in terms of marginal changes: those which are small enough for us to be able to state that the change in satisfaction produced by a change in consumption is proportional to the price. This is equivalent to saying that the change in volume is not sufficient to produce any change in marginal utility for any individual. In cases in which this is not justified a slightly more complex treatment is required and this is discussed in Appendix 1 and also in Chapter 9.

OTHER EXCEPTIONS

On pages 20 to 21, we have seen that a change in the satisfaction of an individual due to a change in consumption of a good or service is proportional to the price paid for it. Furthermore, we noted that the constant of proportionality can be taken as one; this means that collective utility can be measured in terms of market price. Further exceptions to this statement arise when the price paid by the consumer is distorted by special fiscal or financial considerations: two examples may be useful in illustrating this.

Goods supplied to individuals in lieu of salary in order to avoid tax

Due to a penally high rate of personal taxation, many professional people attend unnecessary conferences, entertain each other and their families and accept fringe benefits for which they would be quite unwilling to pay out of taxed income. The difference between the price acceptable to them and the money which is actually paid is a distortion which should be corrected for in any analysis. However, for most economic decisions, this is a relatively marginal factor which would be unlikely to affect the outcome.

Land

Consider a company or an individual buying a block of land or a building of some kind. Suppose that they borrow 70 per cent of the purchase price and borrow the balance at 16 per cent (usuary!). This interest is often deductible for tax purposes and the net cost is therefore in the region of 8 per cent. Suppose further that inflation is 8 per cent; it is fairly clear that in profit and loss terms, that part of the purchase price that has been borrowed costs them nothing. In the case of an individual it may impose a cash drain; however, if that individual is looking for a home for his savings, this is a good one!

The result is that the price actually paid for the land in economic terms is really only 30 per cent of the figure which appears on the conveyance; the balance comes from inflation, (that is, pensioners and so on) and the tax payer. This distortion is very important in many economic decisions and in particular in virtually all planning matters. An example is the recent study of airport facilities in central England in which it was necessary to put a price on airport sites such as Manchester. In this particular case, the market value was in the region of £30 000 an acre, that is £20 000 000 for the 600 or so acres taken up by an average airport. In this case, it could obviously make a great deal of difference whether one took this £20 000 000 at its face value or some reduced figure such as the 30 per cent already mentioned.

Similar considerations arise when considering various forms of urban development. In many cases, planners may be misled by the high market price of land and may take decisions on location, density, and so on, which are wrong from the community's point of view. Because of the importance of this issue, a more extensive discussion of it is given in Appendix 3.

TIME

Up to now we have reasoned in terms of a change which affects only one period of time. In practice this is, of course, seldom the case, and we must now generalize our treatment to cover a number of time periods. Going back to the individual consumer we defined satisfaction as being a function of consumption. Clearly this covers both the present and the future, with the individual introducing a notion of subjective equivalence between any two time-periods.

For example, suppose that we ask him to choose between a change in his consumption worth £100 this year and an equivalent change next year. In most cases he will only prefer the deferred benefit if this is larger in absolute terms than the present one. This is no more than the well known case of 'a bird in the hand'. In order to extend our theory to cover more than one period we must, therefore, find some way of measuring this equivalence. Fortunately there exists at least one market in which this is dealt with specifically — that involving money transactions and interest. When a person agrees to loan £100 at, say, 10 per cent a year for five years, this is equivalent to saying that he values equally the initial sum and the series of payments that it would produce over the five years. In order to equate one with the other he applies a discounting factor of 10 per cent to the interest and the capital repayment and this produces the arithmetical equality which expresses his indifference between the two choices. This subject is discussed further in Chapter 6; for the moment it should be noted that the future can be taken into account by discounting receipts and payments.

TAX

One of the enterprises covered by the analysis on page 22 is the Government in its role as a collector and spender of taxes. However, as this is such a special case, it should now be looked at more closely. In our treatment we calculated the change in profit of all the enterprises in the economy. This calculation included taxes, and as a result the change in collective utility would include a term with on the one side the change in government receipts from tax, and on the other any change in government expenditure. At this point it is often useful to make an assumption which might be called 'the principle of optimal management by government'. This assumes that faced with a change in tax receipts the Government will adopt one of two alternatives.

1 Balance its books and spend any increase in taxation that may be obtained. If it is managing its business optimally such an increase in expenditure will bring the community a benefit that is exactly equal to the change.

2 Adjust rates of taxation so that the total amount received over the entire economy is constant. If this were done any increase in taxation revenue resulting from an economic choice would be paid back to some of the other agents in the economy.

In either case it is fairly obvious that a change in total taxation paid will lead to an exactly equal change in collective utility, and this means that it is immaterial whether we calculate profit before tax or alternatively after tax and then add the tax paid to the collective utility function (the 'profit' of government). For reasons of simplicity of calculation it is very often more convenient to do the former.

An interesting exception to this rule, even if the assumption about optimal management by government is accepted, is provided by the case of unwanted consumption that was described on page 25, illustrated by the example of a bypass. A fairly classical problem is to decide whether the change in consumption of petrol resulting from the construction of such a road should be valued excluding or including tax. This is discussed in the following section.

PETROL SAVINGS FROM A BYPASS

In this example we are faced with the evaluation of a bypass to be built around a town, which will have the result that each journey will consume less petrol. The figures are shown in Table 2.3.

	No bypass	*Bypass*	*Difference*
Passengers	1000	1050	50
Cost of petrol per journey			
Resource cost	10	9	1
Tax	20	18	2
Total	30	27	3

Table 2.3

We assume that the only costs of travel are the consumption of petrol (made up of 'resource costs' such as labour, machinery, etc) and purchase tax.

Suppose that the 'enterprises' in the economy are the Government, the petrol manufacturers and 'others'. We use our assumption of optimal management of business to eliminate effects concerning these 'other' companies; this leaves us with two terms.

1 The profit of the petrol company; here again we can say that profits after tax have been optimized. Thus the profit before tax will have changed by the difference in tax, that is:

$$1050 \times 18 - 1000 \times 20 = -1100$$

2 The savings to the existing passengers; this is a case of the unwanted consumption referred to on page 99. It is worth a $1000 (30 - 27) = +3000$.

The overall saving is thus:

$$-1100 + 3000 = 1900$$

This can be expressed in another way as:

$$100(10 - 9) + 50 \times 18 = 1900$$

The meaning of the two expressions on the left of the equal sign is: (a) the saving in resource costs to existing passengers; and (b) the tax element of the cost of the petrol used by new travellers.

CONCLUSION

We have seen that the expression for the change in collective utility corresponding to an economic decision can be written as follows.

1 The change in profit of all companies before tax.

2 The change in use made of outside resources such as unemployed labour.

3 Any consumption that does not affect satisfaction.

4 An adjustment for cases in which price changes are not marginal.

5 The total change in consumption of non-economic goods such as noise, etc.

All these terms are evaluated at the prices in force before the change implied in the decision.

An important special case arises if the last four are zero; here we see that our expression is nothing more than that used in the day-to-day decisions of individual companies − their profit. There are, however, three important provisos that should be noted.

(a) The profit is evaluated at constant prices; increasing prices may well be in the interest of the company but not of the community.

(b) The calculation is before tax; companies usually take their decisions after tax. (Although not always, surveys carried out in the UK to determine the efficiency of development area tax incentives showed the contrary. Firms said that they 'were not sure' of obtaining the reliefs because of changes in legislation.)

(c) The future is evaluated at an overall risk-free discount rate rather than by attempting to maximize something such as the internal rate of return.

The implications of these three potential sources of divergence between a company's position and that of the community are discussed in Chapter 14.

3

The Short Listing Problem

THE PROBLEM

Even a fairly simple application of cost benefit analysis requires a certain volume of data, and this in turn costs money. Two classes of problem have led to a search for less expensive methods; in both cases the cost of analysis is high compared with the importance of the decision and the resources available.

1 Problems where the data available is inherently poor and difficult to improve. A classical example is the selection of research projects in which it is extremely difficult to quantify the benefits and costs of a project. Furthermore, these total costs are likely to be relatively small when compared with the fixed investment.

2 The early stages of almost any investigation in which some form of short listing is required. The two extremes of such an investigation are the initial retention of ideas and the final detailed analysis using methods of the cost benefit type. The initial retention of ideas becomes almost a question of intuition whereas the final analysis is detailed and relatively expensive. In between we need a method which will provide a rational basis for weeding out ideas without spending too much money.

These two problems are the subject of the rest of this chapter. We will discuss two examples based upon the choice of research projects by an international consultancy group, and the short listing of sites for a regional airport.

SELECTION OF RESEARCH PROJECTS

History

The method to be described was developed for a large international consultancy organization covering, among other things, operational research, computers and some aspects of civil engineering. The organization had a central research department to whom ideas were submitted by the operating units. Once a year the research programme was brought up-to-date with decisions being taken on the rejection of projects which no longer seemed promising and the addition of new ones.

The selection procedure was carried out by a committee made up of representatives of the operating units. They came to the meeting armed with documentation on their projects, and the final choice was arrived at by a mixture of logic, dealing and sheer exhaustion. Not infrequently the resulting selection received less than wholehearted support and it was felt extremely unlikely that it was in the group's best interests or that it made the best use of the data available.

In 1967, a new method of selection was introduced; this aimed at dividing the projects into classes on the lines of Table 3.1.

| | Expenditure | |
Class	Class	Cumulative
1	127	127
2	26	153
3	259	412
4	192	604

Table 3.1

If the budget were, for example, 500, the table would be useful in that it would indicate accepting projects in the first three classes, and perhaps adding one or two from Class four.

The method

The first stage in the classification procedure was to agree on a number of criteria which together described each project sufficiently for the purposes of selection. In this case the criteria given in Table 3.2 were used.

In addition, each project was scored on the basis of its continuity with existing research on a four-point scale (GG – exceptional; G, N, F, FF – unfavourable).

It is worth noting that only two of these criteria are expressed in financial terms, the likely present and future cost. The success of the project is considered to be measurable in terms of the strategic importance of the research to the company, the likely total market available, the probability of technical success and the continuity with existing research. The selection of these criteria was guided

	Favourable	Average	Unfavourable
Strategic importance	SS	SM	SI
Market importance	MS	MM	SI
Probability of success	A	B	C
Immediate cost	1	2	3
Future cost	1	11	111

Table 3.2

by three main considerations.

1 As far as possible they should be independent of one another. For example, in this case there was no point in including a criterion for the time taken to carry out the research as this was very closely related to the cost for the type of project being considered.

2 The final selection had to appear reasonable. This is obviously something that can only be judged after the end result has been produced. However, in earlier versions which excluded continuity, it was found that the procedure led to excessive instability. This has two main disadvantages: dissatisfaction among research workers; and an indirect lowering of the probability of success.

3 The possibility of obtaining a fair degree of agreement on the classification involved. Each project was classified on the three point scale noted in the table, and even this degree of unanimity would have been impossible if the criteria had been expressed in some derivative form, for example, yield on capital, margin per ton and so on.

Having decided on the criteria, and having classified all the projects according to them, the problem was how to proceed further. An initial approach, which is the equivalent of cost benefit analysis, would be to attach values to each score for each criterion. However, in view of the very limited amount of information available, this would have given rise to a totally fallacious impression of accuracy. The approach finally adopted was to use a series of axioms on the lines of the following.

(a)   A loss of one level in any criterion must mean one loss in class.

(b)   The loss of probability from A to B gives a bigger drop in class than a loss of probability from B to C.

(c)   The difference between high strategic importance and medium is less than the difference in class from medium to insignificant.

(d)   The difference between medium and great market importance is also less than medium to insignificant.

(e)   The inequalities in (b), (c) and (d) can only increase as other criteria get worse.

(f)   The difference between great strategic importance and insignificant is greater than the corresponding one for market: strategy more important than market size.

(g)   If the immediate and future costs are small ((a) in each case) the loss in class from A to B is equal to that from SM to SS.

(h)   The loss in class resulting in a change of immediate cost is greater than that for future cost.

(i)   The difference in axiom (h) increases as other criteria get worse.

(j)   There are 20 basic classes; any falling outside this are rejected.

(k)   If there is no previous research the abovementioned axioms give the classification.

(l)   The existence of previous research affects the classification with the exception of Class 1 which cannot be improved upon.

(m)   The change between none and some previous research is less than that between some and an advanced project and similarly in the other direction.

(n)   The differences in (m) increase as other criteria get worse.

These axioms make it possible to build up tables giving the classification of any project with a given score. An example of one of these tables is given in *Figure 3.1.*

It should be noted that the axioms add much less information to the situation than the use of scores, and that in particular it may turn out that all the projects fall into the same class. In this case all that we can say is that the method is not

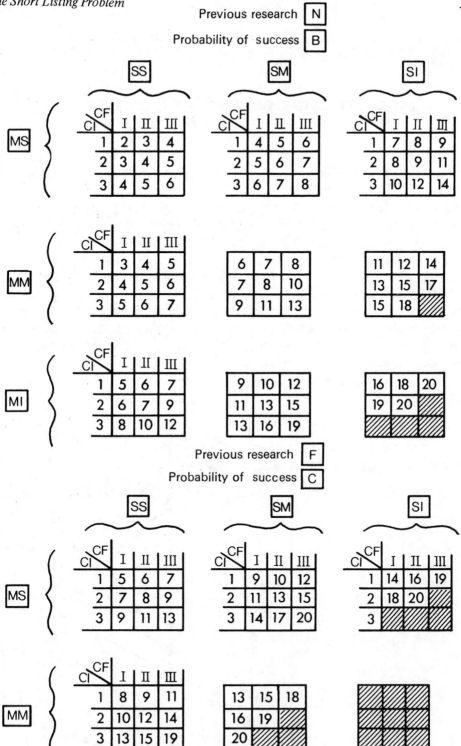

Figure 3.1 *Classification of research projects*

sufficiently powerful to discriminate, and that more information is required.
A more detailed description of this method is given in *Metra* (1968)[2].

THE SHORT LISTING OF AIRPORT SITES: USE OF THE
OUTRANKING RELATIONSHIP

This example is based on a study of regional airport development in the United
Kingdom. It has however been camouflaged somewhat as certain aspects of the
original study were confidential.

The area covered is shown on the map in *Figure 3.2* which covers an area about
100 miles square. The main reason why a new airport was felt to be necessary is
that the existing one (marked A on the map) is some 70 miles to the west and
communications with it are relatively long and costly.

There has been a good deal of talk of developing the existing military airfield
which is marked with a small square on the map. However, mention of this possibility aroused considerable opposition in neighbouring villages and as a result the
Department of the Environment decided upon a full enquiry which was to look at
all sites on which an airport was possible technically. Twenty such sites were
found, and these are also marked on the map (*Figure 3.2*). Without going into a
great deal of detail, it was felt that each of these sites could be fairly easily

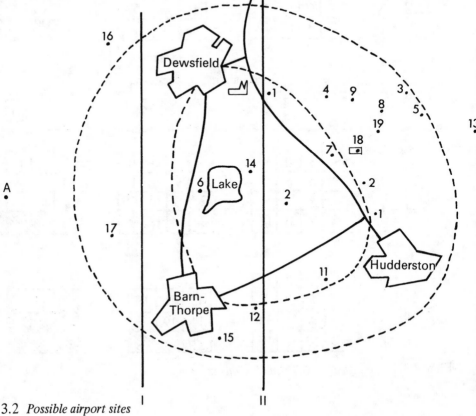

Figure 3.2 *Possible airport sites*

classified according to seven criteria, and that these seven points gave a reasonably good indication as to whether the site would be suitable or not. The criteria were as follows.

Access time	0	Up to 20 minutes by car from a motorway
	1	20 to 40 minutes by car from a motorway
	2	Over 20 minutes by car from a motorway
Access cost	0	In inner contour
	1	In middle contour
	2	Outside middle contour
Noise	0	Noise contour contains no part of a town
	1	Noise contour includes small areas of a town
	2	Noise contours affecting large areas of a town
Defence	0	No interference with defence activities
	1	Air traffic control interference with defence activities
	2	Military site (or closes another military site)
Competition	0	To the east of Line 11
	1	Between 1 and 11
	2	To the west of Line 1
Amenity	0	No identifiable effect on amenity
	1	Only minor effect on amenity
	2	Major effect identified
Construction cost	0	Existing runway with sufficient strength and length
	1	Existing airfield
	2	Greenfield site

The values agreed on for the 20 sites are shown in Table 3.3.

It was felt that the cost of analysing all 20 sites in detail would be excessive, and that it was desirable to produce a short list of four which would then be the subject of cost benefit analysis.

Short listing: Stage 1

The first stage of the short listing process was based on the notion of dominance. This can be illustrated by a comparison between sites 1 and 2. These are the same on all the criteria with the exception of transport time for which 1 is better. This enables us to say that whatever the value of the criteria, site 1 is better than site 2; site 2 is dominated by site 1. If this statement is not immediately obvious, it is only necessary to attach values to the different scores. It will be seen that what-ever non-zero values are used, site 1 will always have a better score than site 2. As we are only looking for one site, this means that site 2 can be knocked off the list which we have thus reduced from 20 to 19.

A little thought shows that in a similar way site 3 can be eliminated as it is

Site	Transport time	Transport cost	Noise	Defence	Competition	Amenity	Capital
1	0	0	1	1	0	2	1
2	1	0	1	1	0	2	1
3	2	1	1	1	0	1	1
4	1	1	0	0	0	0	2
5	2	1	1	1	0	1	0
6	0	0	1	0	1	2	1
7	0	0	1	2	0	0	2
8	1	1	1	2	0	0	2
9	1	1	0	1	0	0	2
10	0	1	1	0	0	0	2
11	1	0	1	1	0	1	1
12	1	1	1	0	1	0	2
13	2	2	0	1	0	1	0
14	1	0	1	0	1	2	1
15	2	1	1	0	1	1	0
16	2	2	0	1	2	1	0
17	2	1	1	0	2	1	0
18	0	1	1	2	0	0	1
19	1	1	1	2	0	0	1
20	0	1	1	1	0	0	2

Table 3.3

dominated by 5, 8 which is dominated by 9, 9 dominated by 4, 12 by 10, 16 by 13, 17 by 15, 19 by 18 and 20 by 10. Thus, it is interesting to note that a very simple concept has enabled us to reduce our long list by 50 per cent leaving us with 10 sites to be considered. However, we had decided that the maximum length of short list that we could treat by a full cost benefit analysis was 4 and it is clear that some new methods must now be used.

Short listing: Stage 2

The procedure described in the previous section can be compared to the voting of a committee. We have put a variety of comparisons to the vote; only when this is unanimous has the motion been carried and the losing site eliminated. Many multi-criteria methods have been inspired by the behaviour of committees, and in this particular case we used one based on two simple ideas.

1 Concord: by this we mean the degree of agreements on any proposition. In this case we stated that concord was present if a majority of the criteria favoured the comparison under discussion. Other forms of concord are discussed later in this chapter.

2 Discord: this expresses the fact that certain comparisons are not possible on the amount of information which has been gathered so far. For example, we examined the consequences of saying that one site could not be declared better than another if the 'worse' site was in fact very much cheaper than the 'better one'.

Table 3.4 shows the comparisons for which there was a degree of concord, that is, a majority of criteria in favour. For example, the tick in the first line under Column 7 means that we could state that site 1 is better than site 7; this is on the grounds that site 1 is better for defence and capital cost, but worse on amenity. Similarly, the tick in the seventh row under Column 5 means that site 7 is better than site 5 because it is superior on the two transport considerations and amenity, although worse on defence and capital cost.

Medium List Comparison

	1	4	5	6	7	10	11	13	15	18
1	—	—	—	—	✓	—	—	—	—	✓
4	—	—	✓	—	—	—	✓	✓	✓	—
5	—	—	—	—	—	—	—	—	—	—
6	—	—	—	—	—	—	—	—	—	—
7	—	—	✓	—	—	—	—	—	✓	—
10	—	—	✓	—	—	—	✓	✓	✓	—
11	—	—	✓	—	—	—	—	—	✓	—
13	✓	—	—	✓	—	—	—	—	—	—
15	—	—	—	✓	—	—	—	—	—	—
18	—	—	—	—	—	—	—	—	✓	—

Table 3.4

The information in Table 3.4 can be expressed in the form of a diagram (*Figure 3.3*). In this we see that no comparison was possible between sites 4 and 10, but that these were both better than 13, 5, 11 and 15 and so on. On the same sort of argument that was used when eliminating sites on the grounds of dominance, we can now say that we need only examine sites 4, 10, 6 and 1. It is fairly clear that we must look at the first two of these; if we do so there is no need to look at sites 13, 5, 11 and 15 as these are all 'dominated'. We do however need to look at 6 and 1. Seven and 18 can be again eliminated as they are dominated by 1.

Suppose that we were now to remove comparisons in which the 'worse site' had a score of zero on capital cost whereas the 'best' one had a score of 2. A number of relationships would be eliminated and our diagram would break down somewhat (*Figure 3.4*). The short list now expands and changes to become 4, 10, 13, 7, 18 and 5.

On the other hand, if we were to say that no comparisons were valid if there

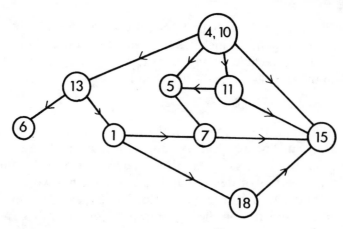

Figure 3.3 *Diagram of relationships – concord only*

was a difference from 2 to 0 on amenity, the diagram is relatively undisturbed and we would only need to add site 15 to the four originally selected. Similarly, if the extreme values on travel time are declared to be incomparable, there is no difference to the short list.

There is no doubt that methods of this kind are far more troubling than the relatively cut-and-dried evaluation put forward in other chapters of this book. However, a number of comments may be useful.

(a) Amazingly good progress can often be made with the notion of strict dominance in which we only retain comparisons that have unanimous support. In this case we saw that a long list of 20 was reduced to 10. Thus the general principal of using a number of criteria without introducing explicit exchange rates is an attractive one and, on the face of it, it is worthwhile to seek extensions of it.

(b) The diagram of relationships gives us a very clear idea of the extent of our knowledge. For example, if we try to be too exigent about the majority needed to prove modified dominance, or if we introduce too many discord functions, the entire diagram breaks down and we are able to make no statements whatever. This means that we either abandon the problem or else spend more money on collecting data. This relationship between the quality of data and the certainty of any statement is basic to decision taking, but it is not always brought out very clearly in analysis. For example, it is quite possible to carry out a cost benefit analysis on extremely poor information, and to produce a table which looks just as convincing as one which is the result of long and painstaking work.

(c) A good indication of the structure of the problem can be given by adding and subtracting constraints and seeing to what extent the short list varies. If it is fairly robust, then one can be reasonably confident; if not, more work is required.

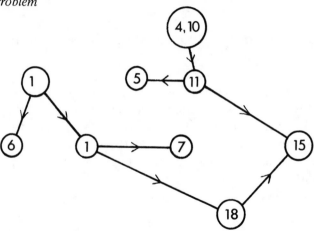

Figure 3.4 *Diagram of relationships — discord or causal cost*

(d) In cases involving a large number of choices, it is often useful to introduce computer programs. A number of these exist which enable the relaxing and hardening of concord and discord functions to be carried out very simply. Among other things, these have been used for the selection of advertising media. This problem presents the characteristic that the different criteria used have widely differing scales (for example the cost per reader is known very accurately whereas the suitability of the media for the message may only be classified on a 10 point scale at best).

CONCLUSION

Most problems of decision involve three stages: (1) the generation and initial selection of ideas; (2) some form of short listing; and (3) a final detailed analysis.

We have seen that in some cases the final detailed analysis is not possible, for example for the selection of research projects. Whether this is so or not, there is a need for some form of technique lying between the intuitive reasoning which decides inclusion in a long list of possibilities, and the detailed study involved in cost benefit analysis, industrial investment, appraisal of the discounted cash flow variety and so on.

A first step in such short listing procedures can often be made by the use of the dominance criterion. This means that if one project is better than another from every point of view, there is no need to relate these criteria together, and in particular no purpose in the introduction of exchange rates expressing them in terms of money or of some other measure. Unfortunately, in many problems this does not however take us far enough, and this has led to the search for methods based on a number of ideas. In this chapter we have examined two.

(a) The use of simple relationships between criteria. We have referred to these as axioms. The most important point to nore is that they add far less information than the use of exchange rates.

(b) The use of outranking criteria which are based on the analogy of the behaviour of a committee.

It is true, however, that in terms of decision one only gets the certainty for which one is prepared to pay. This can rarely be determined in advance. In some cases a relatively simple short listing procedure will be sufficient to eliminate a large number of solutions with confidence. In others, this will not be possible and it will be necessary to increase the budget of resources at this stage or else to take a leap into the dark!

The studies in this chapter are based on theoretical work carried out by le Roy[2].

4

Forecasting

Before any quantification of the results of a decision can be attempted in monetary terms, it is essential that the physical consequences of the choice should be clearly identified. This chapter discusses some of the methods available. It should be realized, however, that whatever the help to be obtained by sophisticated techniques, the production of forecasts is essentially a matter for judgement. For example, in the kind of marketing decision that was referred to in Chapter 1, the whole issue normally depends upon the estimate of increased sales resulting from changes in pricing, advertising and so on.

Having said this, there are a number of extremely powerful tools available and some of these will now be dealt with in turn.

STATISTICAL METHODS

Generally, the future can be assumed to have some continuity with the past. Expressed in graphical terms, most phenomena of any size trace a fairly smooth curve, the slope of which is not subject to abrupt changes. Therefore, statistical analysis of historical data can be extremely useful in forecasting. This analysis is designed to establish correlation between a number of identifiable factors and the phenomenon that we are trying to forecast. For example, the sale of a product may be related to: (1) the population; (2) the average disposable income per head; (3) the number of competitive products and their prices; (4) advertising appropriations; and (5) the time period covered.

By analysing historical sales one may be able to build up a model to forecast the various factors on which sales are alleged to depend. For example, in the case that we have just quoted it is assumed that fairly reliable forecasts of population growth will generally be available. If all else fails one almost always knows the period for which one is trying to forecast.

This analysis of past data in order to isolate a pattern that can be associated with some event in the outside world is sometimes called the analysis of time series; it has been greatly facilitated by the use of well-designed computer programs, as the calculations involved are often extremely voluminous.

Such methods obviously become less applicable the further ahead we look. Although it is almost certain that there will be no abrupt discontinuity in behaviour, this would not be true over a long period. To take a very simple example, consider the growth of air traffic which is now running at about 6 per cent a year; while this rate is likely to be maintained with fair precision over the next three-to-four years it could be extremely unwise to assume that similar growth will last up to, say, the year 2000. Similarly we are very often frightened with statistics concerning the world's population; while it is possible that a continuation of present growth rate could leave each of us with only a few square metre of space, this seems on the whole unlikely.

A specific snare of statistical analysis is the possibility of establishing 'correlations', which are nothing more than the effect of chance. For example, when people first became aware of the link between smoking and lung cancer, quite a lot of ingenuity was displayed by statisticians who demonstrated that equally good correlations could be shown with the consumption of tinned peas and a variety of other oddities.

SCENARIOS

When looking at problems involving long-term development, historical data becomes distinctly less useful; here we are often obliged to go back to first principles and a useful method that has been developed is known as scenarios. This is really a series of disciplined sessions on the lines of brain-storming. For example, consider the long-term demand for transport; one might have the following ideas.

1 Businessmen travel to attend meetings; with vision-phones will it not be possible to organize discussions without people being physically present?

2 Businessmen travel to visit installations; the same remark holds.

3 Tourists travel to see foreign countries; will this interest continue as communications improve and as hotels everywhere become identical?

4 Tourists travel to find the sun; 50 years ago people avoided the sun. Will this situation come back? Will artificial 'suns' (under domes) come to replace the real thing?

The discipline referred to is arrived at by forcing the participants to face up to any logical inconsistencies that their forecasts might expose. For example, in a recent study of the profitability of a motorway project in London, traffic forecasts were produced relating to visits that people would make to their friends in other parts of the city; the rates of rise of traffic were so steep that it seemed likely that many of the journeys would be wasted, as nobody would be left at home to be visited.

Methods of this kind have been used extensively in the preparation of the sixth French National Plan[3]. Exercises were carried out to find the result of a number of basic assumptions on the development of the nation; these included the following.

(a) The possibility that agriculture would be feasible without the use of land.

(b) The possibility of everyone living in coastal towns.

(c) France with 100 million inhabitants.

In each case the planning horizon was the year 2000.

Methods such as this can be particularly powerful if associated with statistical analysis of the kind referred to on page 43.

MARKET RESEARCH

A special case of the analysis of the statistical information is given by market research. Here forecasts are based on analysis of either 'naturally occurring' historical facts or of experiments set up for the purpose. Fairly sophisticated procedures have been worked out by companies marketing consumer goods, and these can be applied to a wide range of problems. For example, if a town is considering closing its centre to traffic, it may be possible to use at least three forms of market research.

1 Analyse what has happened in other similar towns when decisions of this kind have been taken.

2 Carry out a pilot study by, for example, closing the town centre for a period of a few days.

3 Carry out a questionnaire survey asking such things as: 'Would you go there to shop if it meant walking 200 yards?'

All these methods have their advantages and disadvantages and it may be useful to look at some of the more obvious ones.

Analysis of similar situations elsewhere

This has the great advantage that we are able to examine the situation over a period of time. This is extremely important, as reactions to such a scheme will almost certainly vary as people adjust to it. Similar phenomena are observed when looking at people's reactions to nuisances such as noise, pollution and so on.

In most cases those involved become accustomed to inconvenience or unpleasantness, but there are circumstances in which the reverse occurs. For example, they may be prepared to walk from the car park to a new shopping centre, as long as this remains a novelty, but will abandon it once the gilt has worn off.

The disadvantage of such analysis is that no two cases are strictly comparable. A particularly interesting example occurs in consumer goods marketing and in many cases involving innovation, when we attempt to use American experience as a model. Whilst it is likely that we will follow transatlantic customs, there are a number of striking cases in which this is not so; conditions of employment and length of holidays for example.

An artificially designed experiment

Here it will be assumed that the experiment has been well designed in a statistical sense and that analysis of the results should theoretically give useable results. There are of course many cases where this condition is not met. For example, in consumer goods market research it is by no means unknown to find a situation in which two variables are changed at once so that there is no way of telling whether differences produced are caused by a new advertising campaign or a price reduction.

Normally, an essential requisite of such an experiment is the existence of a control; for example, if we are trying to find out whether one pack design is more successful than another, it is important that two similar areas should be chosen with the original pack remaining on sale in one of them.

The advantage of such well-designed experiments, is that they are usually relatively cheap to carry out, and make it possible to isolate the phenomenon under study. However, their disadvantages are that they only represent a small sample of the real world and, more serious, that unless carried out over a long period they are unlikely to be successful in dealing with the kind of changes in attitude that were referred to earlier.

Questionnaires

Once again, a prerequisite of any research based on questionnaires is that the actual questions should be well designed and properly laid out for subsequent analysis. For example, in the shopping centre problem, it is likely that a bald question, 'Would you go there to shop if it meant walking 200 yards?' would receive extremely unreliable answers for a number of reasons.

(a) Asked on the spur of the moment, people simply do not know.

(b) They might be unwilling to admit that such a small effort would deter them, particularly if this could in some way be said to be 'good for them'.

(c) Even if it were possible to measure their genuine attitude at any given moment, it is likely that this will develop over a period.

Such problems can be partially remedied by the careful design of questionnaires, the introduction of check questions and so on; however, in many cases market research has to be taken further by using depth interviews to find out what are the factors that really influence behaviour. In addition to giving indications on which to base forecasts, such an analysis may have the additional advantage that it isolates the reasons for opposition to a scheme. This may then be modified, or, if the opposition is irrational, the information obtained can suggest lines along which advertising might be envisaged in order to overcome the resistance.

BUSINESS PROFITS

As we explained in Chapter 2, it can be assumed that a marginal change in economic activity will have no effect on the profits of most businesses. This profit was defined as being cash income less cash outgoing, taken over a long period. It includes investment in either plant or working capital as an expense when it occurs; in particular the idea of depreciation is excluded.

An example is the position of petrol suppliers in the event of the building of a new motorway which might increase consumption.

1 Many petrol stations will be able to sell the additional volume with existing investment and at very little cost — their gross margin is additional profit.

2 A number of stations will need to undertake major investments (additional pumps) which are not immediately fully utilized; for them the additional sales may well produce a loss in the short term.

3 On average there is no reason to suppose that the margin of surplus capacity will be any different after the change from what it was before.

4 Thus the total effect on the profit of the industry is likely to be zero. This contains the assumption that the yield on capital for the petrol distribution industry is on average the same as the overall discount rate, which is discussed on page 83.

Exemptions to this general assumption are likely to be industries in which there is either spare capacity or substantial possibilities of economy of scale. For example, in the hearings of the Roskill Commission it was assumed that the marginal cost of carrying an additional passenger was very much less than the fare paid — 20p per mile and 2p per mile respectively — thus, in this particular case, any increase in the number of passengers could be forecast to produce a very substantial change in profit

However, one should be on one's guard against the widespread assumption among businessmen that their marginal cost is lower than their historical cost, for example, that they would be able to sustain additional volume without any corresponding indirect expenditure or investment. This has led many firms to accept investment projects that are 'profitable', taken individually, but which lead to an overall loss and also to a widespread belief that 'they' (the central organization) are in some way frittering away the profit that the 'productive units' have earned.

A particularly important point in forecasting business profits is that these are often not materially affected by changes in cost levels but rather by the overall competitive situation. An industry for which a very high percentage of the total cost is represented by raw materials, for example, margarine, will often be able to produce its profit estimates without any specific forecasting of raw material prices; this is because the final consumer price of the company and its competitors is virtually arithmetically indexed to the price of the raw material.

In this example an interesting case arises if the price of the oil used in manufacture rises so high that there is a substantial difference in the competitive position relative to butter. This may well force a squeezing of margins.

For this reason it is often better to concentrate relatively scarce resources on the evaluation of the competitive cituation, rather than on a detailed item-by-item forecast of the profit and loss account.

Industrial location: Rijnmond

In many countries, decisions taken by the public sector concerning industry are based on a very poor appreciation of the economic situation of companies. However, a number of recent studies have made heartening progress in this respect; a particularly encouraging example will now be described; it covers the work of P M H Kendall[4] and his team on behalf of the Rijnmond Authority in the Netherlands.

The Rijnmond Public Authority is a grouping of local Government interests around the Europort in the Netherlands. One of its aims has been to encourage industrial development around the port, and to do this it naturally placed considerable emphasis on the most striking advantages of the area and in particular to deep water sites available to industrialists. This policy appeared to be extremely successful until two things happened.

1 The Port Authorities ran out of deep water sites.

2 It was observed that many of the companies occupying deep water sites were not using the deep water.

The Rijnmond Authority then found itself in the position of having to encourage companies who made little use of deep water to relinquish any further options on sites, thus releasing the land for those industries where deep water represented a genuine economic advantage.

Public authorities are often tempted to view industrial location in such macro-economic terms. Comparisons with other areas are made in terms of cheap labour, good communications, and so on. Even when this very general approach is modified to differentiate between industrial sectors, there is a marked reluctance to go further and look at individual companies. However, the facilities such as deep water may only be of interest to those companies importing sufficient quantities of raw material to warrant the use of very large ships; therefore, the statement that such an asset will attract companies from other sites in Europe must be carefully qualified. After its early experience, the Rijnmond Authority realized that the only sensible way forward was to commission a research programme designed to look at this problem of location in far more detail than had been done hitherto.

The starting point was to find out exactly what motivates industry. After examining industrial location in all its aspects from the point of view of a company, the study began by defining a procedure for evaluating alternative sites. This would determine the extent to which the process could be formalized and quantified, and was designed to enable the local or national authority to understand more closely their potential clients' point of view. To date, the project as commissioned by the Rijnmond Authority and the Dutch Ministry of Economic Affairs represents four and a half man years of effort with two of the three phases completed. The methods used involved the conjecture and test method of interviewing throughout north-west Europe; although principles of location are very different in the various countries, local rules and costs are often different. The outcome so far is a programme specification for a general evaluation routine for any company on any site including present and future annual estimates of all relevant resources.

Major relocation decisions are a relatively rare event even in large companies, and furthermore the final choice may only evolve gradually as a result of a complex process of analysis and decision. This means that interviewing on such a problem must be carried out at the highest possible level in the company, in most cases the chief executive. Furthermore, in order to obtain sensible results a great deal of preparatory work has to be done in advance of the interview; this is what we referred to as the conjecture and test approach. The team responsible for the study must work out a fairly clear description of what they imagine the decision process will be, including at least an outline evaluation of a number of sites from the point of view of a company of the same size and in the same industrial sector as the interviewee. Ideally, this document is then sent to the respondent and the interview based on it. In practice the Rijnmond team found that such preparation

Results from Prototype Eramus/Freight
(All figures are in Guilders)

Refinery Locations Tanker sizes	1 Amsterdam for 6 m tons	2 Amsterdam for 12 m tons	3 Rotterdam for 6 m tons	4 Rotterdam for 18 m tons	5 Delfzijl for 6 m tons	6 Delfzijl for 35 000	7 Schelde piped from Rotterdam	8 Schelde under 72 000 no pipe
Crude oil shipping cost	22.8 m	18.4 m	22.8 m	17.4 m	22.8 m	34.3 m	22.8 m	25.2 m
Cost per ton	3.8	3.1	3.8	2.9	3.8	5.7	3.8	4.2
Annual pipeline cost							5.6 m	
Cost per ton							0.93	
Total crude transport	22.8 m	18.4 m	22.8 m	17.4 m	22.8 m	34.3 m	28.4 m	25.2 m
Cost per ton	3.8	3.1	3.8	2.9	3.8	5.7	4.7	4.2
Distribution Bunker C.	5.2 m	5.2 m	1.0 m	1.0 m	23.3 m	23.3 m	8.3 m	8.3 m
Cost per ton	2.6	2.6	0.5	0.5	11.7	11.7	4.2	4.2
Distribution Ind/ Heating	8.5 m	8.5 m	8.7 m	8.7 m	19.5 m	19.5 m	14.2 m	14.2 m
Cost per ton	2.1	2.1	2.2	2.2	4.9	4.9	3.6	3.6
Distribution domestic heating	10.6 m	10.6 m	10.6 m	10.6 m	10.6 m	10.6 m	10.6 m	10.6 m
Cost per ton	5.3	5.3	5.3	5.3	5.3	5.3	5.3	5.3
Total refined products distribution cost	24.3 m	24.3 m	20.3 m	20.3 m	53.4 m	53.4 m	33.1 m	33.1 m
Cost per ton	4.1	4.1	3.4	3.4	8.9	8.9	5.5	5.5
Total cost	47.1 m	42.7 m	43.1 m	37.7 m	76.2 m	87.7 m	61.5 m	58.3 m
Cost per ton	7.9	7.1	7.2	6.3	12.7	14.6	10.0	9.7

TABLE 4.1

was amply justified for the following reasons.

(a) It gained the interest of chief executives and helped them realize that the research was being properly and intelligently carried out.

(b) It obtained replies of a very high standard.

On page 11, we noted that meaningful comparisons between alternatives can only be realistic if these alternatives are sub-optimized. By this we meant that the scheme relating to each alternative has to represent the best solution possible in each case. This was particularly important when dealing with industrial location as the layout and conception of a factory can be very different according to its location. For example if land prices are high, there will be a tendency to build on several stories. Similarly methods of handling raw materials will be related to the way in which they are transported to the plant, attitudes on labour-saving machinery will be determined by the price of labour and so on. It was therefore essential that the work should take into account such local adaptions.

The factors covered by the model included revenue, raw materials, transport, labour, capital, land, utilities, and costs of construction, conversion and maintenance. To give an idea of the kind of detail which is required when analysing the situation of an oil refinery from the point of view of transport, Table 4.1 gives an example of the kind of data which was analysed.

Conclusions

The Rijnmond Authority and the Dutch Ministry of Economic Affairs wanted to be in a position to negotiate with individual companies in an informed way and to develop a coherent policy for deciding on industrial investment. The study which we have just outlined produced a computer program 'Erasmus' which is capable of bringing together information on a wide variety of costs and of producing an economic comparison between a number of sites. The company wishing to locate in the Rijnmond area, or making out a case for economic assistance to encourage it to do so, is asked to produce a certain amount of standard data. This is fed into the program together with up-dated costs for the Europort area and for the most commonly encountered competitive locations, and a comparison is then produced. This can be discussed with the company very soon after the initial meeting.

The use of the program in determining a regional industrial policy would be to carry out such calculations for a representative range of industries in a number of competitive sites. Such work would produce the following results.

(i) An indication of those industries for which an area had the greatest natural economic advantages.

(ii) An evaluation of the extent of Government assistance which should be offered to industry in order to make an area attractive, and of the form in which this assistance should be provided. The latter is particularly important if the public sector is to avoid handing out money on a plate in a way which does not correspond to the industrialists' real needs.

We have quoted this example as it is one of the very few in which a Government has made a serious attempt to evaluate a complex problem such as location from the company's point of view. The results of such exercises are however vital if cost benefit analysis is to be properly used on issues of this kind.

PRICE LEVELS

We have seen that the collective utility function is calculated by multiplying changes in consumption by prices. In order to do this we must be clearly able to forecast what prices will be. (It should perhaps be repeated that these are the prices in the control solution; we do *not* have to evaluate prices for all the solutions and in particular do not include any terms: '*difference* in price multiplied by total consumption'.) Two interesting cases will be discussed in this section. In both of these, prices expressed in 'real money' are referred to, excluding any effect of inflation. This is discussed further in Chapter 6.

Salaries

In many industrial decisions it is vital to have a specific estimate of how salaries will develop. The most obvious example is when considering whether to replace a manual operation by a mechanized one. More generally salaries must be estimated because other factors are proportional to them, for example, the value of leisure time.

It is usual to evaluate gross salaries and to relate them to such things as the overall economic development of the country concerned. However, when looking at some forms of consumption, the appropriate figure is salary net of tax, and this may be of particular importance when forecasting such things as the consumption of luxury goods. In this case a difficult aspect may be forecasting income tax rates.

Excluding these difficulties it is usually reasonable to suppose that gross real salaries will increase at the same rate as industrial productivity – between 3 and 6 per cent a year depending upon the country concerned.

Industrial goods

The price of industrial goods with a high labour content should normally decrease in real money terms. A striking example over the last fifty years is provided by the motorcar. Similarly in the example of a motorway crash barrier quoted in Chapter 6, the cost of replacement is assumed to be less than that of the original installation.

In an industrial situation the timing of the introduction of automated plant is often decided by two opposing trends: the fall in the real cost of the plant and the rising price of labour.

The rate of technical improvement in any given case must be the object of specific study. For many well-established products with a 'normal' mix of labour and other costs it is not unreasonable to assume that prices will stay fairly constant in real money. However, for new industries or ones in which there is little labour, price falls can be very substantial indeed.

ATTITUDES OF PEOPLE

Values of leisure time are often related to salary. This is also commonly assumed to be true for other intangibles such as noise, comfort and so on. However, this relationship may well vary as attitudes change. To take the case of noise, it may well be that people will become more tolerant to this nuisance as it becomes more widespread; if so, present-day objections to such things as airports could disappear in future. Conversely, attitudes could develop in a way similar to those relating to smell; until the nineteenth century this was regarded as something quite unavoidable and therefore to be endured. Attitudes were only changed when medical discoveries led people to regard smell as being an intolerable nuisance that should be eradicated even if this involved considerable expense. We may shortly see a similar development relating to sea pollution, which until recently was regarded as something of a joke.

The importance of attitude is, of course, well known in a consumer marketing context; here it gives rise to extremely difficult problems as soon as one attempts to look at long-term developments. For example, the long-term success of prepared food products, and particularly convenience foods, depends upon the cultural attitude towards eating. This could well lie anywhere between the vast meals known in the nineteenth century and the adoption of a daily (or weekly) pill.

WORKING HOURS

The length of working hours is an important factor in the evaluation of time. When looking at business time, the cost of an employee has got to be spread over the number of hours worked in order to arrive at a value. Equally, when looking at leisure time, the relationship with salary is determined not only by the problems of attitude that we have already mentioned but also by total working hours.

It is generally assumed that working hours will tend to decrease and that the increase in productivity referred to on page 52 will be passed on partly in the form of greater leisure.

5

Quantification of Forecasts

The analysis in Chapter 2 showed that the economic terms fell into three categories which will now be dealt with individually.

The change in business profits

This has already been discussed in Chapter 4. Computation is greatly facilitated by the use of our 'optimal management' assumption.

The change in the consumption of outside resources

Here we will consider two examples: external trade; and changes in unemployment.

External trade

An increase in imports improves the satisfaction of the community in the year in which it occurs; it is a benefit. Similarly the diversion of goods to export represent a 'loss'. This may appear surprising as we are accustomed to consider things the other way round, and to regard an improvement in the balance of payments as a good thing and a deterioration as the reverse. This paradox is rather similar to the one concerning investment and consumption, raised in Chapter 1. In the case of the balance of payments, increases in imports usually involve some degree of sacrifice for the future. Looking at a sufficiently long time-span, the temporary advantages produced by a deterioration in the balance of payments will, therefore, normally be cancelled out when this is 'paid for'.

A similar situation is, of course, true when looking at a personal overdraft. In both cases the money can be used either for present consumption, in which case an immediate advantage is paid for later, or for investment, in which case the proceeds may, or may not, be big enough to pay off the loan.

It is often reasonable to assume that even in the short term the Government applies some form of balance of payments policy and that any 'gain' in imports in one year will be offset by an unidentified loss elsewhere. For this reason such changes can often be ignored. However, as with the tax assumptions mentioned in Chapter 2, the way in which the balance of payments are treated will depend upon the nature of the problem analysed. For example, when looking at a relatively limited investment decision the overall assumption 'balance of payments constant' may be perfectly appropriate, whereas clearly this would not be true if one was studying an export deposit scheme, the prime aim of which was to affect the balance of external trade.

In some studies it has been suggested that a deterioration in the balance of payments should be 'weighted'. In some circumstances this could be appropriate and notably if the short-term situation were a matter of considerable preoccupation for the Government or alternatively if the conditions applicable to overseas loans were substantially worse than our overall discount rate.

Unemployment

A project may affect the level of unemployment, both present and future. This is often true for such things as public works in a depression situation, and was quite correctly exploited by pre-war German governments for building motorways. In such cases the wages paid to people who would otherwise have been unemployed are not a resource cost from the point of view of the community and should therefore be removed from the overall evaluation of the project. The following example illustrates this.

Land reclamation project.   We want to know whether it would be worth while reclaiming an area of marsh land in order to build houses. The differences between reclaiming and not reclaiming are shown in Table 5.1.

The following comments can be made on this analysis.

1 The total net profit position of the various enterprises concerned becomes worse as a result of the reclamation. Therefore, normally, one would conclude that this was not a worth-while project.

2 The project would, however, employ labour costing £3000 which would otherwise not have been used (compare the example on page 22 in which the labour saved by the food manufacturer was absorbed elsewhere in the

	Owners of swamp	Reclamation company	Building industry	Other industry	Total
Unreclaimed land	500	(500)	–	–	–
Reclaimed land	–	2000	(2000)	–	–
Labour	–	(2500)	(500)	–	(3000)
Other plant etc.	–	(500)	(500)	1000	–
Shooting	(50)	–	–	–	(50)
Houses	–	–	3000	–	3000
Other consumer goods	–	–	–	(1000)	(1000)
Profit	450	(1500)	–	–	(1050)

Table 5.1

industry).

The usual treatment in such a case is to add back the cost of this labour and to say that the adjusted position is not the overall loss of 1050 but a gain of 1950. In this case the gain is represented by the additional houses that will be available less the 'other consumer goods' foregone (including shooting!).

3 The adjustment just suggested assumes that the individual unemployed persons will not suffer any disadvantage from having to work; this is, however, by no means obvious, and to this extent the traditional analysis is open to criticism. In particular, if their needs are covered by fairly generous unemployment pay, they may be by no means enthusiastic about the reclamation project in question. However, in general, the dissatisfaction produced when an unemployed man is given a job is probably very much smaller than the amount he is paid and may even be negative for reasons of self respect.

4 The item of 500 shown on the line 'unreclaimed land' could represent compensation. It should be noted that the analysis is unchanged whether or not this compensation is paid. This is an example of the principle that transfer payments can be ignored in such an analysis. The situation would, of course, be different if the owner of the land were not a member of the collectivity whose welfare we are studying but were, for example, a foreign company.

Consumption which brings no satisfaction

It has been shown that the satisfaction of individuals is determined by the consumption of a certain number of goods and services, providing these are defined widely enough. However, in some cases this relationship is not a direct one. For example, in the case looked at in Chapter 2 concerning building a bypass, the service that was appreciated by the consumer was not the consumption of petrol but the accomplishment of a given journey. If the quantity of petrol required for this journey were to be reduced by a better road scheme, this would not have any effect on the satisfaction per journey. Therefore, one should be on the look-out for such cases and modify the analysis accordingly. A number of interesting examples arose in the hearings of the Roskill Commission and these are discussed in Chapter 8. They generally arise when an individual is obliged to undertake some changes in expenditure.

INTANGIBLES

For the purposes of this chapter, intangibles, which are sometimes called socio-economic goods and services, are defined as those things which affect the satisfaction of individuals but for which no economic market exists. Examples are time, environment, standards of health, level of education, comfort and so on. Partly because of the absence of a formal system of prices, such intangibles have often been given less attention than the more traditional economic goods and services that enter into the profit and loss accounts and balance sheets of companies and governments. However, the absence of a market in such things as noise is more apparent than real. For example, when a man buys an expensive motor car, rather than a 'banger', one of his reasons may be that the engine is so quiet that the only noise is the ticking of the clock. Similarly, the situation of a house being in peaceful surroundings may well add to its value considerably. The readily identified object that is being purchased is a piece of land and the building standing upon it; however, the absence of noise, smell, vibration, and so on, or the presence of an attractive view, may be just as important in determining the price as the quantity of bricks used.

There is rather a strange paradox about attitudes to intangibles such as the ones just mentioned. On the one hand, they are sometimes described as the most important things in life, implying that the health of our children, the peaceful quiet of a summer's evening or the smell of the wind from the sea are of far greater importance than mere monetary considerations. On the other hand, we behave as if many of these items did not exist in the same way as 'real' property.

When an urban motorway is built, compensation is paid to those who lose the bricks and mortar of their dwellings, whereas those whose peaceful summer evenings in the garden have been replaced by the roar of traffic receive nothing. Similarly the 1949 Civil Aviation Act[5] expressly excluded claims for compensation from airlines for the noise caused.

One of the claims of cost benefit analysis is to reconcile these two attitudes by introducing a realistic system of valuation for items of this kind. The rest of this chapter considers a number of specific cases.

Time

The amount of time available to an individual can usually be taken as constant. The only real exception is in the study of health programmes designed to prolong human life. The more general problem is to compare different uses of time.

In spite of a certain amount of interesting theoretical work by economists such as Becker[6], applications here are often primitive. It has been found useful to study time from two different angles: the point of view of the individual and that of the business when looking at the working time of its employees.

Time spent by an individual

Individuals can spend their time in a wide variety of different ways, most of which involve the consumption or production of economic goods and services. Examples are as follows.

1 Working for wages.
2 Walking in open countryside.
3 Driving a car so as to get to the open countryside.
4 Going to the theatre.
5 Waiting in a queue to obtain a theatre ticket.
6 Travelling to go on holiday.
7 Sitting in a dentist's chair.

Time spent in any of these ways has an effect on the satisfaction of the individual; an interesting category of economic problem concerns decisions which will enable time available for leisure activities to be increased by saving time on less-attractive pursuits. The following are some examples.

(a) Building motorways to make travel by car quicker so that more time is available for playing golf, walking, or general holiday occupations.

(b) Construction of supersonic aircraft with similar aims in mind.

(c) Introduction of high-speed dentists' drills so that the time spent in an extremely painful situation can be reduced.

(d) Introduction of sophisticated booking systems, perhaps based on computers, to reduce the waste of time in theatre queues, searching for an hotel, booking an air ticket and so on.

Looking at these examples, it is fairly clear that there is no one 'value of time'. What is meant is a system of prices that an individual would be prepared to accept in order to replace one use of time by another. He would presumably be prepared to pay more to avoid five minutes in the dentist's chair having a tooth drilled by a slow machine than to obtain service five minutes quicker in a restaurant with an attractive view. This means that it can be extremely mis- leading to use values of time obtained in one context for the evaluation of 'savings' in another.

A useful concept in practice is that of general leisure time. By this is meant the average net satisfaction obtained by an individual from time, the use of which he can freely determine. In evaluating a road scheme, the use to which the traveller will put any time saved is probably not defined; it can be referred to simply as unrestricted leisure.

An initial estimate of the value of such unrestricted leisure time can be obtained by considering the equilibrium with working time. Many people have the possibility of working longer and earning more. This may be in a very immediate sense as in the case of a worker who can choose to do overtime or not, or a professional man who can accept one more client or not. However, it can also apply in the rather longer term to most salaried workers; they often have the choice between accepting a new job involving longer working hours and better career-prospects, or alternatively staying where they are. Such people could therefore increase their unrestricted leisure time by working slightly shorter hours and by sacrificing a small amount of income. This small amount is the net marginal rate for their job. In the case of a manual worker this would be the overtime rate less the marginal rate of taxation.

It would not be surprising, therefore, if people who were given the possibility of saving time in situations that are rather similar to work — such as waiting in a queue — were prepared to pay approximately 70 per cent of their net hourly income in order to replace one hour of this unwanted activity by one hour of unrestricted leisure.

A field in which considerable research has been carried out is that of saving commuter time. This involves exchanging the mildly unpleasant conditions of commuter journeys for an equivalent amount of unrestricted leisure. In specific cases this may mean that the commuter can get up a little later, arrive home in time to read a bedtime story to his children, be in time for the beginning of a dinner party, and so on. A wide variety of European studies have shown that commuters are prepared to pay about 25 per cent of their gross income in order to save time in this way. These studies are listed and analysed in an interesting paper produced by Harrison and Quarmby[7]. Similar studies carried out in North America and in particular by Thomas C Thomas[8] in Chicago have shown rather higher percentages of the order of 50 per cent. These differences may be an interesting example of the influence of attitudes that was described in Chapter 4.

The methods used for obtaining these values of commuter time fall into two main categories.

Traffic surveys. The traditional example of a traffic survey to determine values of travelling time is that of a ferry replacing a long land journey around the head of an estuary. In this case observations can determine what percentage of the population is prepared to pay the ferry toll rather than spending the time driving.

However, this is an obvious case in which time is by no means the only consideration; many people derive considerable enjoyment from driving along the river and others from the ferry trip across it. This defect is common to almost all traffic surveys; it is extremely difficult to isolate time from other factors, such as comfort or handling luggage.

Very much more sophisticated studies using this same principle have been carried out on commuters; a classic case is the one analysed by Thomas in Chicago[8], where he observed the number of people prepared to pay a toll on a motorway rather than use the slower alternative road system. Other studies have been based on the number of people prepared to use their private car rather than public transport; however, this is a case where questions of comfort and psychological attitudes may well be just as important as time.

The results obtained from these commuting studies have been used in a number of other contexts. However, there is a clear need for further work in order to obtain values applicable to such things as waiting in queues. This is, of course, a very common problem in the organization of many forms of service.

Market research. A variety of market research techniques have been used on the evaluation of time; these are built around more or less sophisticated versions of the question: 'If a faster means of travel were available at such and such a price would you use it?' The advantage of such methods is that they make it possible to isolate the factor of time from other considerations; however, they suffer from the defect of all questionnaire market research – the statistical significance of the end result is open to some question. In consumer goods marketing it is notorious that the most difficult questions to answer are those concerning price.

A fairly typical example of such market research was the study carried out by Metra, and published as part of the British Airports Authority's evidence at the hearings of the Roskill Commission[4].

Linearity of time values

An interesting question in the context of many traffic schemes is whether the valuation of time is linear – that is, are twelve savings of five minutes worth as much as one saving of an hour? Although a great deal of argument has been produced to demonstrate that short time savings are relatively worthless, no very convincing evidence is available one way or another.

A good working assumption, therefore, is that the value of such small time savings is proportional to that of larger ones. While it may be true that on some occasions a small period has virtually no value, equally there are times when it can have very important results, such as missing a train or deciding to travel a day later.

People without earned income

Time values are usually expressed in terms of earned income. This obviously presents a problem in a number of cases and in particular when dealing with housewives. A number of studies have assumed that the valuation of leisure time for such women should be equal to that of their husbands and the following arguments can be used to support this.

1 Housewives clearly have an economic output even if this is not expressed in terms of money; it is represented by such things as the various services they perform in the home, giving birth to children, and so on.

2 Women could perfectly well perform most of the functions that men do. The fact that society prefers them to act as housewives and mothers implies that these services are on average valued equally highly as those of men.

3 The average hours worked by housewives are also probably on average equal to those worked by men.

4 It follows that a woman's time, and in particular her leisure time, should be valued as if she were earning the same salary as her husband.

Further problems are posed by children and students. In the case of small children it is extremely difficult to produce any conclusive arguments. However, some studies, including the Roskill Commission[1], have used a third of the time values appropriate to adults. In the case of students who could otherwise have been working for money it seems a reasonable assumption that society attaches as much value to their efforts as to those of people who are employed; this implies that they should be treated in the same way as other people of their age-group who are in employment.

Business time

Business time is a resource like any other and it can be valued at the price which a business pays for ir. This is on the assumption that at the margin a businessman produces exactly what he costs. Two specific problems that arise are the cost of time and the amount that is lost.

What is the full cost of a businessman? Figures have been suggested between two and three times the gross salary paid and a possible breakdown might be as follows.

	£
Salary	3400
Superannuation	350
Accommodation	850
Secretary	1200
Profit	1000
	6800

Value/hour based on 2000 hours/year 3.40

When applying these figures to small time savings a number of interesting questions arise.

1 If a businessman is prevented from working for a certain time, it is fairly clear that his salary and the direct cost associated with it, such as his pension, are lost. However, is this also true of his secretary's time, the cost of his office space, and so on? In most cases the answer is probably yes, as office space and secretarial assistance are generally provided so as to be sufficient to deal with the executive's full-time requirements. Furthermore, it is comparatively rare that such resources are efficiently used during a business-man's absence. However, there may be organizations in which an empty office is promptly turned into a meeting room, and in which secretaries work an effective pooling system, so that someone whose boss is away on a journey is not reduced to reading and knitting.

2 The profit element that is shown corresponds to the yield on the company's capital. It is, of course, arguable to what extent this is dependent upon the effective action of management. However, even if we accept this, it would not normally be correct to take into account any further profit, even if the overall action of an individual manager produces a surplus that is in excess of his total cost. At least, in fairly large organizations, it can be assumed that the staffing of management positions is such that at the margin the value of the manager's services is exactly equal to his total cost; including a reason-able return on the capital for which he is responsible.

When is time lost?   In many cases the mere fact of being absent from his office, may mean that a manager's time is totally lost as far as his employers are con-cerned. However, in other cases the situation is more complicated; it may be that someone is capable of working quite hard in a chauffeur-driven car, a train or an aeroplane. Equally, many businessmen claim to do a great deal of business over lunch, at conferences of different kinds, and so on. It is, unfortunately, extremely difficult to obtain any very convincing objective evidence on this point; as in the case of the uses of leisure time, the way in which a final evaluation is arrived at is clearly very specific to the exact comparison that is being made and will vary greatly according to the way in which the time is lost.

In some circumstances a businessman may catch up part of the time that he has lost, thus effectively converting the loss from one of business time to one involving his own leisure. Although many businessmen appear to believe the contrary, such catching up is not very realistic particularly in circumstances where the loss is caused by conditions over which the businessman has no control, for example, a longer air journey because of the use of a slower aircraft.

The notion of unavoidable time losses is worth a comment. Anyone involved in an activity which is not simply routine is bound to lose a fairly high proportion of his time for a variety of reasons; he may be disturbed by something having nothing to do with the job, wasting time looking for papers, and so on, or simply not being in the mood to carry out a certain job. Most of us have days on which we feel that we have achieved very little and others which are extremely productive. However, although the unproductive part of the time may be relatively easily identifiable in retrospect, it is literally impossible to avoid it. The situation is rather analogous to Lord Leverhulme's famous remark about advertising; 'I know that half of what I spend is wasted; I don't know which half'.

A rather interesting analogy is the situation within a company in which a department is expected to absorb a little more activity without extra staff. In such circumstances businessmen often assume that it will be possible to deal with one extra client or one additional product without increasing indirect expenses. However, assuming things are reasonably well organized before this additional burden is placed upon them, such hopes are usually shown to be extremely un- realistic other than for a very short-term effort; if the increase in activity is material, expenditure is usually incurred and the total relationship between indirect expenses and sales remains more or less constant.

In the same way a businessman faced with a short-term additional load may well be prepared to increase his working time in order to deal with it. However, if he is faced with a loss of time that enters into his working conditions, it is likely that there will be a general redistribution of costs and that his total output will go down. A fairly striking case is that of a salesman who finds that the journey from client to client takes longer because of a deterioration in traffic conditions. It is likely that his daily work load will be reduced in order to take this into account.

OTHER INTANGIBLES

This section will cover a number of other intangibles that are appearing with increasing frequency in cost benefit analysis.

Noise

In the same way as for leisure time, it is most important to define the exact nature of the noise and the circumstances. Music that might be delightful in a concert hall can be most annoying, even at a low level of volume, at two o'clock in the morning coming from a neighbouring flat; similarly the noise of a sports car may be exhilarating to the driver but most unpleasant to those whose houses are near the road.

Quite a high level of constant noise is often less worrying than an intermittent slight one; an example is the effect of someone trying to get to sleep to the sound of a rushing stream or a dripping tap.

Ideally measures of noise should contain at least four components.

A measure of the energy level of the noise when it is present

This is often expressed in terms of decibels and Table 5.2 gives an illustration of a few typical noises.

Noise Level of Some Typical Sounds

Noise sources of environment	Sound level (dBA)
Room in a quiet London dwelling at midnight	32
Soft whisper at 5ft	34
Men's clothing department of large store	53
Self-service grocery store	60
Household department of large store	62
Busy restaurant or canteen	65
Typing pool (9 typewriters in use)	65
Vacuum cleaner at 10ft in private residence	69
Inside small saloon car at 30 mph	70
Inside small sports car at 30 mph	72
Inside small sports car at 50 mph	75
Inside compartment of suburban electric train	76
Ringing alarm clock at 2ft	80
Loudly reproduced orchestral music in large room	82
Printing press plant (medium-size automatic)	86
Heavy diesel-propelled vehicle about 25ft away	92

Table 5.2

This table is expressed in decibels using a sound level meter with A weighting (dBA). Experiments carried out for the Wilson Report[9] showed that the difference between these decibels and the perceived noise decibel (PNdB) referred to in the discussion of aircraft is approximately: PNdB $-$ dBA = 13.

For example, an aircraft producing 130 PNdB (this was classified by the Wilson Report[9] as very annoying) would score about 117 dBA.

A description of the noise involving its pitch

It is well known that human beings are not capable of hearing the full range of noise, and it is, therefore, likely that even quite intense noise at some frequencies cannot be classed as a nuisance at all. However, it is equally true that some frequencies are far more annoying than others even within the audible range; for example, it is often stated that piston-engined aircraft are less disturbing than the high-pitched whine of a jet. Equally the staccato barking of a dog may be far more troublesome than the lowing of a cow even if this is of equivalent intensity.

Various indices exist including the PNdB[10]. This weights together the sound levels of different frequencies so as to give more importance to those to which people are most sensitive.

The profile of the noise over a period of 24 hours

Noise is generally far more troublesome at night, but no very satisfactory way has yet been found of incorporating this into an index. It is, however, interesting to note that at a number of airports night flying is seriously restricted, and that it would, therefore, be inappropriate to use a measure derived from daytime readings if the level of nuisance were in fact to be very different at night.

In the same way as for time, measurement techniques fall in two categories: observation of actual behaviour and market research. In the first category most work has been done on house prices; however, this is extremely difficult to interpret for the reasons discussed below.

The frequency with which the noise occurs

For example in the case of road or air traffic this would correspond to the number of movements. To deal with this the usual measure employed is the noise and number index (NNI); this is defined by the following equation (Reproduced by courtesy of the *Journal of the Town Planning Institute*[11] which also contains an interesting discussion of other measures.):

$$NNI = PNdB + 15 \log N - 80$$

where N is the number of aircraft heard on an average summer day between 07 00 and 19 00 hours (BST) and PNdB is the average peak noise of these aircraft in PNdB. The following examples (Table 5.3) describe typical NNI levels[10].

Values for noise

A number of methods have been used to derive values for different levels of noise nuisance, such that these could be used in cost benefit analysis. We will discuss three of these; measuring the depreciation of houses, market research and a noise machine experiment.

Depreciation of houses

As we saw on page 58, people pay for the absence of noise in a variety of circumstances and in particular when they buy a house. This has led a variety of researchers, including the Roskill team, to try and measure the depreciation of houses as a result of the imposition of noise; they then equate the result

NNI (refer to daytime 06 00 – 18 00 hours except where stated)	Social survey around Heathrow (for Wilson (Committee 1963)	Surrey CC planning restrictions
8	Average reaction 'not at all annoyed by aircraft noise'.	
32	Average reaction 'a little annoyed by aircraft noise'.	
35 (night)		As for 50 NNI by day
40		Above this level refuse major housing developments; allow infilling
42	Average reaction 'moderately annoyed by aircraft noise'.	
45 (night)		As for 60 NNI by day
50		Above this level no infilling except with insulation
60	Average reaction 'very much annoyed by aircraft noise'.	

Table 5.3

with the nuisance suffered by some statement on the lines of 'average nuisance suffered is equal to the average depreciation of houses'.

Unfortunately, a point that was not sufficiently appreciated was the fact that the depreciation of houses depends not only upon people's subjective attitudes to noise, but also upon the relative supply of noisy and quiet houses. (House prices are also of course influenced by a very wide range of other factors; in particular it should be noted that houses near airports can, under some circumstances, increase in value if people attach greater importance to the benefit obtained in terms of employment, better services, access to travel, and so on, than to the disadvantages of noise. This is similar to the position in suburban London where access to a railway station is regarded as a considerable asset.) If there are relatively few quiet houses in an area, the difference in value between noisy and quiet ones would be much larger than if most houses were quiet. This is no more than the scarcity value of the tranquility obtained. The Research Team assumed that this phenomenon did not exist and that the average depreciation in house values was in some way equal to the average nuisance inflicted on the population.

This situation can perhaps be illustrated by a simple example. Suppose that houses can be divided into two categories, noisy and quiet, and that people are of two types, sensitive and insensitive. Equally suppose that the total population of the area considered is typical of the population at large and that it contains 20 per cent of sensitive people. Further let us assume that 10 per cent of the houses change hands each year.

First, consider the situation in which half the houses are noisy and half are quiet, say 5000 in each category. In any year 1000 people move out, and the 1000 newcomers who replace them are made up of 200 who are sensitive to noise and 800 who are not. Obviously the 200 will have no difficulty in finding quiet houses to suit them as there are 500 in this category on the market. Thus the premium for quiet houses is likely to be very small and could even be zero.

Now take a second situation in which there are only 5 per cent of quiet houses; this could correspond to a rather industrial area with a large number of main roads, railways, and so on, here a quiet house would be something of a find. There would still be 200 sensitive people looking for quiet houses but there would only be 50 on the market; this would clearly lead to considerable competition, with the most sensitive and well-off purchasers bidding up the price. In such a situation there is almost no limit to the premium that might be generated.

An example of this latter situation is the market for houses or flats with gardens and open terraces in intensively built up cities like London or, even more, Paris. These commonly demand very large premiums over equivalent accommodation without these advantages.

Market research

The research that we will now describe was carried out by S P C Plowden[12] on behalf of the British Airports Authority during the Roskill enquiry. The main stages of the work were as follows.

Endurance costs.   A social survey was carried out to assess endurance costs. It was considered that to ask a direct question about the compensation that people would require if some noise were imposed on their neighbourhood, might arouse an emotional response. People were asked, therefore, to imagine that they were moving house and to indicate the sum of money that would represent what they would pay for a dwelling which met all their main requirements. They were then asked to consider houses resembling their ideal, except for one single characteristic which might be regarded as a defect. Finally, they were asked how much cheaper this deficient house would need to be before they would consider buying it.

Eight different houses were described, five of which had defects not related to the subject of the study (for example, that the kitchen was too small to eat in) and three of which suffered from noise of various degrees. These three descriptions were as follows.

Noise and number index

1 Close to a major airport so that
conversion is often interrupted   above 50 NNI

2 One is very close to a motorway;
there is no danger but the heavy
traffic goes on day and night   45–50 NNI

3 One is a few miles from a major
airport; conversation is never
interrupted but on some occasions
one may have to concentrate to
hear what people are saying   below 45 NNI

The differences indicated by the respondents were corrected by the extent to which they had quoted houses more expensive than the one in which they were living. However, apart from this they were taken to be a true representation of the noise nuisance suffered.

Various modifications to this basic method have been suggested; some of these involve 'giving' the respondent a certain sum of money and a certain number of costed components for a house. He is then allowed to play a game in the course of which there is a trade-off of money against nuisance.

Dislocation costs.   Dislocation costs would be borne by each owner occupier who decided to leave an area on account of noise. They were estimated by means of questions in the same survey as we have used to establish endurance costs. The relevant questions were preceeded by a number of enquiries on how respondents liked their present area. These were intended to introduce the subject to the possible move and to provide a consistency check.

For owner occupiers the wording of the relevant questions was as follows.

1 Suppose you discovered that house prices in this area were higher than prices in similar areas five or more miles away. Say, that in those areas you could get a house comparable to this one and make £100 profit after all expenses, would you seriously consider moving?

If no ...

2 What would the difference in price have to be to make you seriously consider moving?

State £

If 'would not consider it at any price' ...

3 You mean that if your house would fetch twice as much as those in other areas you would still not consider moving?

Removal costs and falls in house prices.   These costs were estimated from interviews with experts.   For the fall in house prices resulting from noise, two hundred estate agents in the South-East of England were selected for a postal survey.

Evaluation.   Basically a householder in an area exposed to noise nuisance is faced with two costs.

1 The endurance cost.

2 The moving cost; this is equal to the dislocation costs plus the loss in the value of the property.

In calculating values for noise nuisance, it was assumed that householders would choose the situation which corresponded to the lesser of these costs.   This means that if the value which they attach to noise nuisance is greater than the cost of moving, they will indeed move.
The values resulting from this exercise were as shown in Table 5.4.

NNI	Total noise costs per house
Greater than 50	£2500
45 – 50	£2030
35 – 45	£1500

Table 5.4

Although this research was carried out with great care, it is obviously open to the criticism that the answers given only relate to highly theoretical questions. As we have noted earlier, this is true of most market research. However, before dismissing the conclusions on these grounds, it should be remembered that a great many industrial decisions are based on precisely this form of data.

Noise machine

A number of public enquiries on issues involving noise have shown that the values derived from market research are not acceptable politically.   This is partly because many politicians have only a very sketchy idea of the efforts and skills which goes in to well designed research of this type; however, it also derives from the simple fact that no money actually changes hands and that the results are therefore bound to be theoretical. A possible way of overcoming this difficulty would be to simulate the noise effects of an airport or other source of nuisance in an actual market situation. Tapes would be made of the noise, and people would then be asked to accept a machine in their house for a certain length of time; this would play the tape continuously. To reward them for accepting the nuisance, respondents would be offered a certain sum of money. This sum would be fixed in advance and the only option would be to refuse to accept it; clearly bargaining would distort the situation. The sum would be paid to those who did in fact leave the machine switched on for the stipulated time.

It would be necessary to repeat the survey with different samples of respondents offering a different sum of money to those in each sample. The proportion of people who successfully completed the experiment would be recorded, and this would be plotted against the sum offered to see how the willingness to live with noise increased (as it presumably would) according to the inducement offered. In this way the endurance cost of the particular noise would be established.

A programme of work based on this idea is now in progress; however, it is too early to be able to include any statistically valid results in this account.

Application of noise values

Until comparatively recently noise was regarded as something of a joke. It was, for instance, not uncommon to make fun of someone who happened to be deaf. However, this situation is rapidly changing and a large number of decisions can only be arrived at correctly if noise is properly taken into account.

Specification of housing and blocks of flats

The problem is particularly acute for the construction of internal walls.

Specification of office blocks

In particular the decision whether or not to install air conditioning. This problem is caused by the fact that natural ventilation by opening windows is impracticable because of outside noise levels.

Road traffic legislation

It is increasingly becoming accepted that traffic noice can only be controlled successfully at source. In order to overcome the objections of various economic interests, it is necessary to place a proper value on the nuisance caused to people with houses near roads.

Construction of noise barriers on urban motorways

The only way of damping down noise is by introducing heavy walls and these are of course extremely costly.

Siting of major transport investments

An outstanding example was given by the Roskill Commission, on the siting of the Third London Airport; this is discussed at some length in Chapter 9.

Hours of working of various industrial processes

A particularly interesting example concerns construction sites, where the community has become increasingly intolerant of night working unless methods can be developed of building more quietly.

Design and specification of many forms of plant, household appliances and so on

Pollution

Pollution can take a wide variety of different forms of which the following are examples.

Smoke in towns

Thanks to fairly rigorous control there has recently been a great improvement in the atmospheric conditions in many Western European towns as far as visible smoke is concerned. One way of attaching a value to this nuisance is to calculate the cost of cleaning buildings at some reasonable frequency and to establish some relationship between a certain quantity of smoke and the degree of dirt deposited. This is an interesting example of a technique that is fairly common in economic analysis and which will be referred to several times in this book, that is, what value can be implied from the community's actions? In this case because the community cleans buildings at a given frequency, one can derive a value for pollution.

Of course such an answer does not provide any guide to how frequently one should carry out a cleaning process. This depends upon the value placed by the community on a clean building. Presumably this value could be determined by some form of market research.

In this example it was assumed that the only effect of smoke is to dirty buildings. However, it might be possible to demonstrate some effect on health; in this case an appropriate evaluation should, of course, be added.

Gas pollution

Many towns have introduced restrictions on the percentage of sulphur dioxide present in the atmosphere. This is the result of fears concerning both health and the effects of corrosion on buildings and other articles. However, in order to be able to arrive at a coherent policy in this respect it is very desirable to attach monetary values to different concentrations of this gas and to take action accordingly, perhaps in the form of a tax related to the number of cubic metres released.

Pollution of rivers

Some measurement of pollution of rivers is required if sensible decisions are to be taken concerning the treatment of effluent of various kinds or even the location of population. Measurable effects to which values can be relatively easily attached are the costs to local authorities of treating drinking water, the effect of smell on the value of local houses, and the result on commercial or leisure fishing. In the case of the latter an evaluation can be obtained by measuring what people are prepared to pay to fish a given stretch of water; this is usually largely made up of travelling expenses to get there and some form of fishing licence.

Polluted sea

A large number of disturbing articles have been published on the health hazards of bathing in the sea[13]. Once again the value to a consumer of being able to go bathing can be calculated from observations on distances travelled or on differentials between the cost of accommodation near the sea and that inland.

Attitude of citizens towards the law

Many public decisions involve the introduction of regulations of one kind or another. These can have a number of consequences and in particular the creation of a new group of 'law breakers'. An example, which is discussed in Chapter 13, concerns traffic offences. In evaluating such regulations an important consideration is the attitude of the community towards people who do not comply with regulations other than out of pure self-interest. This is a field in which very little research has so far been carried out but which would merit further study.

The existence of considerable differences in possible attitudes towards the law can be illustrated by the way in which, say, non-payment of taxation is regarded in different countries.

Other factors

So far serious quantification has only been attempted for a fairly limited range of intangibles with work being concentrated on time and noise. However, if cost benefit analysis is to avoid being regarded as an inadequate tool covering only part of the story, it must be extended to deal with all the material consequences of a decision. This will mean attempting to quantify such items as the following.

General amenity

The problem of general amenity is one of the most difficult to quantify. A variety of techniques have been used, however.

1. The market price of agricultural land is usually well in excess of the economic value of the agriculture. In some studies the balance has been assumed to be due to amenity.
2. Activities that can be easily transferred can be valued as the cost of removal.
3. In the case of activities that it would be difficult to transfer, an estimate can be made of the commercial value or of the total amount paid by participants by way of membership fees, and so on.
4. Historic buildings open to the public can also be valued on the basis of the amounts that people are prepared to pay to visit them.

Although it has proved extremely difficult to find better ways of valuing these different assets, there is no doubt that past techniques could be greatly improved.

In a discussion of such questions, however, it must be borne in mind that any evaluation finally decided upon, while representing enlightened opinion, should not necessarily correspond with the views of an over-sensitive minority. This is of course an extremely delicate democratic question; however, the research director of the Roskill Commission quite rightly warned the Commission of the danger of assuming that middle or upper-middle class values were necessarily worth more weight than those of other sections of the community. In particular he noted that any assumptions that such values would be adopted by the whole population should be subject to fairly careful scrutiny.

Comfort

A possible method was sketched out by Foster and Beesley[14] in their Victoria Line study; this is discussed in Chapter 13.

Health

A certain amount of theoretical work has been carried out by J Lesourne[15] and others. However, far more research needs to be done on the definition and quantification of states of health.

Education

This problem may perhaps be illustrated by a recent visit to a university which had just introduced a new 4-year course. The aim of this is to enable students to follow both an arts and a science course. However, when one of the tutors was asked to produce some justification of his contention that 'this was obviously a good thing', he was unable to do so and the whole discussion was rendered extremely difficult by the lack of an accepted framework.

6

The Present and the Future

SUBJECTIVE EQUIVALENCE

Having made forecasts of the various physical results of a decision year by year and quantified them in terms of money, there remains the problem of expressing these annual sums in a single figure covering the whole of the period affected.

Chapter 1 described how businesses use discounting as part of their normal procedure for evaluating investments, either to produce an internal rate of return or a net present value. Similar problems of relating the future to the present arise in public decision analysis, and here too discounting is an appropriate tool. To understand how a financial concept such as interest rate can be applied to the range of terms that have been discussed, including such intangibles as noise and pollution, the behaviour of the individual must be reconsidered.

The aim of the community has been defined as maximizing the satisfaction of individuals, and in Chapter 2, it was shown that changes could be evaluated by measuring differences in consumption in any given period. In theory, one could then go on to look at the problem of time in one of two ways.

1 Widen the definition of individual satisfaction to take into account present and future consumption. To do this we would need to find an expression for the equivalence between the future and the present *for each individual;* this could be described as a personal discount function.

2 Calculate the change in collective utility year by year, and then relate future requirements to present ones by a system of equivalence acceptable to the

Circulation of Annual Cost/Benefit

Year	Traffic million vehicles/year	Accident rate/100 million vehicle miles	Accidents/100 miles	Value of an accident (£000)	Savings (£/mile)	Cost (£/mile)	Benefit (Disbenefit) (£/mile)
0	–	–	–	–	–	5000	(5000)
1	5.0	2.00	10.0	6.8	680	330	350
2	5.5	1.92	10.6	7.1	750	330	420
3	6.0	1.84	11.0	7.4	810	330	480
4	6.6	1.76	11.6	7.7	890	330	560
5	7.3	1.70	12.4	8.0	990	330	660
6	8.8	1.64	14.4	8.3	1190	330	860
7	10.3	1.56	16.1	8.6	1380	4330	(2950)
8	10.8	1.50	16.2	9.0	1460	330	1130
9	11.3	1.44	16.3	9.3	1520	330	1190
10	11.8	1.38	16.3	9.7	1580	330	1250
11	12.4	1.34	16.6	10.1	1680	330	1350
12	13.0	1.28	16.6	10.5	1740	330	1410
13	13.7	1.24	17.0	10.9	1850	330	1520
14	14.4	1.18	17.0	11.3	1920	330	1590

TABLE 6.1

community. This would be a collective discount rate.

In either case the problem of establishing expressions for subjective equivalence between the future and the present is made much easier by the existence of a system in which people and groups trade present outgoings for future gain and vice versa; this is the money market. Here lenders are prepared to equate £100 today, £110 tomorrow, and so on, over a wide range of periods and risk situations.

The interest rates ruling on this market are therefore a measure of the subjective value attached by groups or individuals to future payments and receipts and it seems reasonable to apply them to our satisfaction functions even when these are not expressed in traditional economic terms.

In the Roskill Commission, and elsewhere, there has been considerable criticism of the application of financial discount rates to things like noise nuisance. This is, however, to misunderstand the nature of the process; the problem is to establish a system of subjective equivalence between the past and the future — the money market is only used as a way of determining what numerical values would be applicable.

In order to determine the relationships corresponding to the two alternatives quoted above, it would therefore seem appropriate to look at the rates at which individuals, on the one hand, and governments, on the other, are prepared to lend and borrow. In practice, of course, there is only one market and this means that the two approaches suggested are likely to be roughly equivalent.

EXAMPLE : MOTORWAY CRASH BARRIER

The following example, which concerns the building of a crash barrier on a motorway, illustrates a number of points arising out of the treatment of time. The proposal is to put up a metal fence costing £5000 a mile to build and £330 a year to maintain; this will prevent vehicles from crossing the central strip of the motorway and thus reduce accidents from this source, which are now running at two per hundred million vehicle miles on the road concerned. The basic forecasts are shown in Table 6.1.

Before going on to the discounting process, the following aspects of the forecasts should be noted.

1   The basic information is the traffic forecast; there is growth of 10 per cent a year for the first four years followed by a more rapid increase in years five and six because of the construction of a new town; after year seven, the growth rate falls back to 5 per cent a year. As this is clearly a key assumption, the final decision should be based on calculations covering a variety of such forecasts; however, only one of these is given.

Discounting Costs and Benefits

Years	Net (cost) benefit*	5% Discount factor	PV	10% Discount factor	PV	15% Discount factor	PV
0	(5000)	1.00	(5000)	1.00	(5000)	1.00	(5000)
1	350	0.95	330	0.91	320	0.87	300
2	420	0.9l	380	0.83	350	0.76	320
3	480	0.86	410	0.75	360	0.66	320
4	560	0.82	460	0.68	380	0.57	320
5	660	0.78	510	0.62	410	0.50	330
6	860	0.75	650	0.56	480	0.43	370
7†	1050	0.71	750	0.51	540	0.38	400
Total 1–7†	(620)		(1510)		(2160)		(2640)
7‡	(4000)	0.71	(2840)	0.51	(2040)	0.38	(1520)
8	1130	0.68	770	0.47	530	0.33	370
9	1190	0.64	760	0.42	500	0.28	330
10	1250	0.61	760	0.39	490	0.25	310
11	1350	0.58	780	0.35	470	0.21	280
12	1410	0.56	790	0.32	450	0.19	270
13	1520	0.53	810	0.29	440	0.16	240
14	1590	0.50	790	0.25	400	0.14	220
Total 7–14	5440		2620		1240		500
Total 1–14	4820		1110		(920)		(2140)

TABLE 6.2

*From Table 6.1   †Excluding capital costs of replacement   ‡Capital costs of replacement

2   The accident rate caused by vehicles crossing the centre line is assumed
to be going down by about 4 per cent a year. In such a case data taken
from overall traffic statistics should be carefully examined; a situation
could exist in which accidents were going down (per million vehicle miles)
whereas the rate for the individual road might increase, for example,
because of intensive utilization of all three lanes.

3   The value of an accident has been taken at the level then currently used
in the UK; however, it seems likely that the element due to the loss of
life is undervalued.   Of course, an average of all different types of
accidents resulting from these causes are being considered, whether they
involve death or not.
        This value is assumed to be increasing by 4 per cent a year in real terms
in line with increases in income. As will be noted when dealing with the
choice of interest rates, it is usually less confusing to work in constant
money excluding the effect of overall inflation rather than in current
money – the actual values measured in £s for the years in question.

4   The barrier has a life of seven years; it is assumed that replacement will
be cheaper than £5000 in real terms because of technical improvement.
This is a fairly common phenomenon which is masked, however, by
overall inflation in most people's calculations.

The last column gives the net benefit or disbenefit from the building of the
barrier, year by year – in this simple example it is assumed that there are no
economic or socio-economic terms to be considered other than the value of
accidents and the building and maintenance of the barrier. This annual figure
must now be expressed as a 'present value'; we are determining how much the
series of receipts and payments is worth to the community. This is done in
Table 6.2 which calculates present values (PV).
    The mechanics of the operation are to multiply each annual benefit/disbenefit
by a factor which, in this case, is taken from normal discount tables at 5 per cent,
10 per cent and 15 per cent respectively. Two particular assumptions which
could be noted are as follows.

(a)   The formula for the valuation of future costs and benefits in year n is
the sample geometric function:

$$\frac{1}{(1+i)\ n}$$

where i is the rate of interest; this assumes that the same rate is valid from
one year to the next – an assumption supported to a certain extent by the
behaviour of the money market.

(b)   The same factor is applied to all costs and benefits in a given year. It has been argued that this is incorrect, since all items involve different degrees of risk and that, therefore, it would be more appropriate to use a series of different rates. While there is no denying the theoretical attractiveness of this idea, experience leads one to reject it and to prefer sensitivity analysis using one rate of interest; of course this analysis will reflect the different degrees of risk attaching to various terms. (Sensitivity analysis is the re-calculation of the result using a variety of slightly different assumptions on such things as level of sales.)

The results of the calculation are summarized in the following matrix (Table 6.3).

	Discount rate			
	0%	*5%*	*10%*	*15%*
1st 7 years	(620)	(1510)	(2160)	(2640)
14 years with replacement	4820	1110	(920)	(2140)
2nd 7 years	5440	2620	1240	500
14 years without replacement	8820	3950	1120	(620)

Table 6.3

This looks at the present value of the project at four different rates of interest and in particular the following.

(i)   The justification for the period up to the first replacement of the barrier; this period would not show a net benefit at any rate of interest; it should, however, be noted that the change from 5 to 15 per cent almost doubles the deficit.

(ii)   The whole 14 years with replacement at the end of seven years; it would be impossible to justify the investment at 10 per cent, although it would be acceptable at 5 per cent.

(iii) The second seven years would produce an attractive investment even if one were to use a rate as high as 15 per cent. It is interesting to notice that if we had only looked at the evaluation of the 14 years, we might have concluded that it would be right to build the barrier now; this is only so because the 'package' of 14 years is made up of one very profitable part (the second seven years) and one very unprofitable part.

(iv)   Finally, we have looked at the position if the barrier were to last for 14 years without replacement. Here we see that the project would be accept-able at 10 per cent but not at 15 per cent.

In cases of this kind the question is often not whether to build or not, but rather when to do so. In this case, the first year in which it would be profitable to build a barrier with a seven years life using an interest rate of 10 per cent would be year four.

RATES OF INTEREST

There are, of course, a large number of rates of interest and yields on the market. In 1970 the British Government told local authorities to use 4 per cent (real money) to evaluate housing and 10 per cent (real money) for other purposes; banks may lend at 8 per cent (current money), pawnbrokers at 20 per cent and holders of individual shares may expect 20 per cent after tax. Equally, however, there are companies that make no yield at all.

These differences stem not only from different definitions and levels of risk but also from differences in personal preference.

Any rate of interest that is chosen for cost benefit analysis must, therefore, be an average concept and will probably include a certain element of arbitrariness. However, it is not too difficult to identify a long-term rate of interest, free from undue risk and inflation. If a particular industry has a yield well above this average in any given year, there will be other industries, or perhaps firms in the same industry at different stages in their lives, who will be below it.

In practice, it is usually appropriate to adopt something close to bank rate for low-risk projects and a rather higher rate if the element of uncertainty is greater. It is, however, extremely desirable that the Government should give guidance on this subject, for example, the British Treasury's ruling that 10 per cent is appropriate for nationalized industry.

This 10 per cent is applicable to costs and benefits expressed in constant money. It is usually easier to carry out calculations excluding overall inflation and in particular, this avoids differential movements (such as changes in the cost of building barriers or the value of accidents) being lost in overall inflation. Whichever practice is adopted it is vital that the discount rate and the figures to which it is applied should be on the same definition.

7

Weighting Terms

PROBLEM OF WEIGHTING

Chapter 1 included a very simple example of public decision involving the imposition of a speed limit. This resulted in various costs and benefits to different members of the community. In this example the terms were simply added together and it was tacitly assumed that the State was prepared to accept the present price system as a basis for evaluation. This assumption must now be discussed and to do so a look must first be taken at the general problem of political choice.

POLITICAL CHOICE

Discussions of political choice often begin with the classical paradoxes of group behaviour and, in particular, the intransitiveness of group preferences. (If a person, or group, is faced with three possibilities A, B, C and prefers A to B and B to C, he is said to be transitive in his choice if he prefers A to C.)

Such phenomena were investigated by the Eighteenth Century philosopher Condorcet and others (an example is given in Appendix 2) and arise because individuals are likely to classify a range of possible situations in a wide variety of different ways. This is because of the following.

1 The interests of individuals are different; for example, a person whose house is next to a motorway may feel rather differently about motorway con-

struction than someone who lives several miles away.

2 People's information is different; in the case of a motorway the opinion of a
man who knows where the road is going to be built may be different from
that of his neighbour whose information system is less efficient.

Even if all the members of the group were to agree to base their opinion on what
was good for the community, and even if they were all to agree on the underlying assumptions and be equally informed on the various aspects of the
decision, there would still be a certain divergence of opinion because of personal
views on things like risk. However, the problem would clearly be simplified, and
it was striking that in the discussion of the report written by the Roskill Commission Research Team, considerable unanimity was reached (at least in private) on
what the decision should be.

In the rest of this chapter, it will be assumed that these difficulties have been
overcome and that the decision is being taken either by a single well-informed
person or by a group of such people who have been persuaded to forget their own
individual interests and look at the problem from the community's point of view.

We will first consider a decision affecting two groups of people, those in
development areas and those living in 'other' areas. A number of possibilities are
shown in *Figure 7.1*.

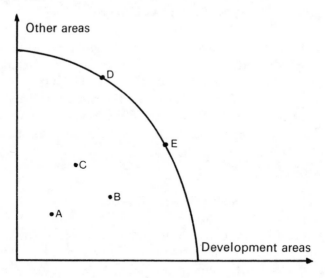

Figure 7.1   *The interest of two groups of people*

The two axes represent the interests of these two groups; each point is a
possible situation resulting from a political choice. When comparing C with A, or
B with A, there would, of course, be no problem; the positions of both groups
of people would be improved by choosing C and B respectively. However, the
choice between B and C is far more difficult; although C would make people in
other areas better off, this would be at the expense of development areas.

There is, however, a limit to the ways in which the Government can improve the position of both sectors of the population simultaneously; this is determined by such things as external trading conditions, the present state of the economy, and the rate of technological progress. This limit can be represented by the curve which encloses all technically possible solutions. The aim of Government policy is, firstly, to be sure that the economy is functioning at a point on this boundary curve and, secondly, to make the essentially political choice between such points. Situations at the limit of what is technically possible, such as D and E in the diagram are sometimes referred to as optima in the sense of Pareto; at such a point the position of one section of the community can only be improved at the expense of some other section.

DISTRIBUTION OF INCOME

We came across the problem of political choice in the development of a collective utility function in Chapter 2. There we found that the change in utility was a linear function of the changes in satisfaction of all the members of the community. (Something is said to be a linear function of a number of variables if it can be determined by multiplying each of these by a constant and then summing the resulting terms.)

The constants in this function were a measure of the importance attached by the community to an individual, and we assumed that they were equal. This was equivalent to saying that the community had no preference between giving an extra £1 to one individual rather than another; we described this as the optimal distribution of income. This assumption is normally a reasonable one if two conditions hold.

1 The social order has reached a fairly stable state. This would not be true if, for example, the Government were in the process of introducing measures such as heavy new taxation on higher incomes so as to redistribute income.

2 The problem being considered is not primarily concerned with social questions concerning the redistribution of income. For example, in considering the introduction of a system of grants to encourage industry to go to development areas, this might only be justified by giving some additional weight to the interests of people in such areas. By definition the overall situation after the application of such a scheme would be worse in purely economic terms than if industry had been allowed to follow normal profit considerations and locate itself more efficiently.

The first of these considerations is almost always met in developed economies; There is practically no body of serious opinion that wishes to further redistribute income and is in any position to do so. The second is also fulfilled by the vast majority of public investment decisions such as the design of towns, the building of a transport infrastructure, the location of public investment such as airports, and so on. A case in which there was considerable discussion of this aspect was the location of the Third London Airport and this will be discussed in some detail in Chapter 9.

Governments in developed countries have at their disposal a wide variety of means of redistributing income; these include taxation, subsidies of various kinds, family allowances, and so on. In a period of social stability in which the first condition is met, it can, therefore, be assumed that the resulting distribution of income corresponds to the wishes of the majority – it is in some sense optimal.

APPLICABLE METHODS

If the assumption of optimal distribution is not accepted, this has very wide reaching effects on the analysis. In particular the transformation of the consumption of individuals into business profit, that was carried out in Chapter 2 is no longer possible. This means that even if the other conditions referred to in Chapter 2 are met (that is, no other economic effects, or intangible factors and profits evaluated in constant prices) the most profitable solution is not necessarily in the common interest. For example, consider the effect on the operation of a taxi service; in this example we have assumed that taxis are used by wealthy members of society and that the community only values their changes in satisfaction at 50 per cent of the value of a corresponding change in satisfaction of a taxi driver (Table 7.1).

	Normal profit analysis	Weighted analysis
Fare paid	20	10
Taxi driver's time	(10)	(10)
Petrol etc.	(5)	(5)
Profit/loss	5	(5)

Table 7.1

The comparison in Table 7.1 shows the normal profit analysis that would be carried out by a taxi driver to decide whether to carry an extra passenger or not and a weighted analysis to take into account society's preference for the satisfaction of the two parties concerned. The following points should be noted.

1   The passenger obtains a certain satisfaction out of his journey for which he pays 20p. Society has, however, decided that this is not a fair measure as he 'ought not to have so much money'; it decides therefore

to value this satisfaction at 10p.

2   In order to allow the passenger to travel the taxi driver has to give up a certain amount of leisure; this could correspond to the fact that he would otherwise have gone home. In this case society accepts the valuation that he puts on his time (10p).

3   In order to carry the extra passenger the taxi driver has to buy additional fuel. We have supposed that this would otherwise not have been produced and that the only result is that a whole succession of other individuals, of similar standing to a taxi driver, do a little less work. Obviously this is a considerable simplification and we could have assumed that the only change was in the revenue of a rich oil sheikh to whom the community might attach no importance whatever.

The result of this move away from the generally accepted pricing system, is that the additional journey, which would have been profitable, is no longer justifiable. It is easy to see that a similar reasoning would apply to any case in which a relatively lowly-paid worker performs a service for someone richer.

It is not uncommon for underdeveloped countries to ban the import of 'luxury' items. This leads to a situation in which the richer members of the community have nothing to spend their money on. Their purchasing power is thus effectively reduced. The reasoning behind such a policy would well be expressed in terms of the kind of weighting that we have just applied.

If society wishes to benefit or penalize some section of the community relative to others, and if for some reason or other it is not able or willing to do this directly by taxation, the following steps must take place.

(a)   The effects of each decision on the different classes of the population must be calculated. Some idea of the complications that this can introduce was given in the brief discussion of the taxi driver's petrol. In particular, we can no longer carry out the convenient transformation of personal consumption into business profits and then eliminate a large number of movements under the 'optimal management' assumption.

(b)   A clear system of priorities must be established, preferably by the Government.

(c)   These priorities must then be expressed in terms of the weights to be applied to the various terms in the analysis. For example, it might be decided that all benefits accruing to people over the age of 65 years should be doubled; this would be equivalent to saying that the Government thought that the incomes of all such people ought to be increased substantially.

EXAMPLE : BUILDING AN APPROVED SCHOOL

This example concerns a local authority that wishes to construct an approved school for juvenile delinquents; two sites have been proposed, one on a green field site in an industrial area, the other involving the conversion of two large houses in an expensive residential area. There has been considerable local opposition to the second possibility, as owners of surrounding houses feel that this would make the area much less attractive for them and that in particular they would not feel safe if there were any possibility of inmates escaping. The local authority would prefer the conversion solution as it would cost them less money and as it is claimed that the improved environment would make it easier to treat the detainees. The situation is summed up in Table 7.2.

Construction of an Approved School: Weighting

	Unweighted analysis (£'000)		Weighted analysis (£'000)	
	Build	*Convert*	*Build*	*Convert*
Profit of local authority				
Construction/conversion	(200)	(100)	(200)	(100)
Purchase of land/houses	(10)	(50)	(10)	(50)
Benefits	250	270	250	270
Owners of land and houses on site				
Loss	(10)	(50)	(7)	(38)
Compensation	10	50	10	50
Owners of houses off site	–	(100)	–	(75)
Total	40	20	43	57

Table 7.2

Conventional analysis shows that the new construction would be the best solution. The following points should be noted however.

1   Even including a purchase price which fully compensates the owners of land and houses on the site, the conversion would cost £60 000 less than the construction of a new school.

2   Benefits arising out of the treatment of inmates have been calculated based on the improved 'success rate' expected by experts in the field.

3   As a result of surveys and the consultation of professional opinion, it has

been established that houses of the quality surrounding the proposed residential site would lose £1000 in value; as 100 houses would be affected the 'conversion' site has been charged with £100 000.

The Government could decide that the valuation placed by the (rich) owners of the expensive residential houses overestimated the importance which society should attach to their loss; therefore, in the evaluation these figures were reduced by 25 per cent and the result is shown in the right-hand part of the table. This shows that the conversion project would now be viable.

The dangers of such interventions in the normal system of pricing are evident however; they include the following.

(a)   The possibility that the administration will decide on the solution that it prefers and then choose a system of weighting that justifies it.

(b)   The use of an economic decision, such as the siting of an approved school, to redistribute income is highly inefficient and lacking in selectivity. Two cases of this can be seen in the present example.

(i)   The owners of large houses in the area considered may have very little in common. They could include a group of old people who have bought modestly-priced flats in one house, the large family of a businessman who has decided to devote an unusually high proportion of his income to housing in another, a wealthy old bachelor in a third, and so on. It seems highly unlikely that the Government would wish to adopt an identical treatment for each of these groups.

(ii)   If the intention were to be to penalize owners of large houses in attractive neighbourhoods, irrespective of their other circumstances, it seems unlikely that the Government would be willing to limit action to the 100 households affected by the approved school. Logically they should adopt some measure, such as increased rates, that would affect all individuals in the community in a similar position; if this were to be done the owners of houses affected by the present scheme would then be penalized twice and this would be clearly unfair. If no such action were to be taken, this would not only throw considerable doubt on the Government's alleged system of priorities but would also be extremely unfair to those people who happened to be near the site in question. In general terms it can be stated that redistribution of income can be more efficiently achieved by direct action aimed specifically at the groups which the Government wishes to benefit or penalize rather than by the distortion of economic decisions.

COMPENSATION

In the example just given, owners of the two houses to be converted were compensated for their loss, whereas those in neighbouring properties were not. However, the analysis would give identical results if this situation were to be reversed − that is, if no compensation were to be paid in either case or if all losers were to be indemnified. This is because the method ensures that all losses incurred by members of the community are identified; the effect of the payment of compensation is to transfer these losses from one section of the community to another. Compensation is one of the transactions that is traditionally referred to as a transfer payment and quite properly the result of the analysis is unaffected by it. Strictly speaking only true on a marginal change.

The proper payment of compensation is, however, a matter of considerable importance for two reasons. First, it ensures that the problem of weighting raised in this chapter does not arise; if losers are compensated at market prices it is not necessary to compare the benefit of those who gain from the decision with the losses of those who are penalized. Second, compensation helps ensure unity of interest among the various members of the community and goes a long way towards obtaining general acceptance of decisions that are in the public interest. This point is discussed again in Chapter 14.

UNITY OF INTEREST

A common feature of many public investment decisions is the emergence of a passionate group of opponents to them. The building of an urban or rural motorway (for example, the London Motorway Box) or an airport (the Roskill Commission) is the signal for vigorous fund raising activities the aim of which is to finance opposition to the project in question. While part of such opposition is based on excessively conservative attitudes, a regrettably large proportion is fully justified; those who are about to suffer know that they will not be compensated. It is common for a garden taken for road widening schemes to be valued at agricultural prices, even if the effect on the market price of the house is very much greater; often those suffering from noise, pollution, and so on, have no redress at all. A great deal of time wasted on opposition could, therefore, be saved if every citizen were to be sure that any losses that he might suffer would be made good by way of adequate compensation. Here it is interesting to distinguish between two cases.

1   Those in which some sections of the community lose relative to their present situation. An individual who has just invested in a house may see his capital disappear as a result of a government decision.

2   Cases in which individuals incur no loss relative to their present position but nevertheless feel that they have been discriminated against. A

common industrial example is that of workers who demand a share in the greater prosperity, resulting from, say, improved working methods, automation, and so on. In the context of cost benefit analysis, similar cases arise in which it is important that people should feel that they have a proper share in future growth or improvements in standards of living resulting from a certain economic policy.

As people's attitudes to various forms of nuisance tend to be highly individual, it is inevitable that any reasonable system of compensation will overcompensate others. However, if this is accepted it should not be too difficult to find a far more equitable system of public compensation than the one at present ruling in the United Kingdom and many other countries.

Part Two

Cost Benefit Analysis in Practice

8

Procedures and Layout of Cost Benefit Analysis

THE ROSKILL COMMISSION

In this chapter and in the one following the deliberations of the Roskill Commission on the Third London Airport will be used as an example. First, the general procedure and layout of the analysis will be described; Chapter 9 then looks at a number of the specific problems that were raised by it.

The Roskill Commission, composed of economists, planners and experts in other fields, was set up by the British Government in 1968 under the Chairmanship of a judge, the Honourable Eustace Roskill. It was asked: 'To inquire into the timing of the need for a four-runway airport to cater for the growth of traffic at existing airports serving the London area, to consider the various alternative sites, and to recommend which site should be selected'[16].

The Minister also suggested that the Commission should use a cost benefit analysis.

After a number of preliminary stages the choice was narrowed down to four sites which were analysed in detail: Cublington, Foulness, Thurleigh and Nuthampstead (*Figure 8.1*).

In order to carry out this analysis the Commission set up a Research Team the preliminary conclusions of which were published early in 1970. The team has continued to advise the Commission during and after a series of public hearings at which the various interested parties were allowed to express their views and to cross-examine one another and the Research Team. In the course of these proceedings, which took place between April and August 1970, a number of alternative analyses were produced.

Figure 8.1 *Third London airport – short listed sites*

This presentation, which is an application of the methods so far described, uses substantially the figures put forward by the Commission in their final Report. However, it does not follow their layout for the reasons that will be discussed in Chapter 9; essentially these are that the Research Team proposed no very complete model and in particular did not positively identify the profits of business as terms to be taken into account.

IDENTIFICATION OF TERMS: COLLECTIVE UTILITY FUNCTION

There is considerable merit in adopting a fairly set procedure for the identification of the terms that have to be studied in the final analysis. It is often helpful to do this in the form of a diagram of the relationships between the various parties involved; this can be progressively extended until two things happen.

1 One has obtained a fairly clear grasp of the problem.

2 The graphical presentation becomes too cumbersome and it is desirable to go over a matrix terminology.

The first diagram used was as shown in *Figure 8.2*. Points to note in this diagram are as follows.

(a)   It started with the organization running the airport at the centre of the diagram and working outwards.

(b)   The boxes referred to various businesses and classes of consumer; 'other

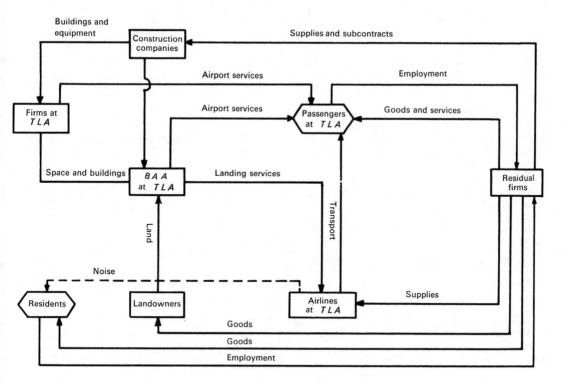

Figure 8.2 *Identification of terms*

businesses' were included and the elaboration of the diagram was essentially the process of moving people in and out of these 'others' categories according to the likely size of the effects concerning them. When in doubt rather too many terms were included and preliminary calculations carried out on them; the items finally retained were the subject of fairly extensive research.

Using this method the terms in Table 8.1 were arrived at.

Profits

Classic profit calculations are required for the British Airports Authority, (BAA), British Rail (BR), airlines and airport services and a number of public bodies concerned with roads and defence. The effect on the profit of general business as a result of time losses to businessmen and the profits from the agricultural use of the land taken for the airport should also be calculated.

Unwanted expenditure by individuals

This covers the removal costs of those who are obliged to leave their homes, the

Economic terms	Cublington	Foulness	Nuthampstead	Thurleigh
Profits				
BAA Construction	18	50	14	–
Other	5	–	2	1
BR Capital	3	26	12	–
Other	–	(75)	(15)	(14)
Airlines	–	9	35	30
Airport services	23	–	17	7
Public bodies Roads	–	4	4	5
Defence	29	–	5	61
Other	12	–	29	33
General business	–	157	41	38
Agriculture	–	3	4	2
TOTAL	90	174	148	163
Unwanted expenditure by individuals				
Removal costs	–	–	–	–
Journey costs to airport	–	88	18	17
Journey to work	–	–	–	–
TOTAL	–	88	18	17
Intangibles				
Time	–	46	9	9
Noise	20	11	73	14
Amenity	12	–	11	7
TOTAL	32	57	93	30
TOTAL COST/BENEFIT	122	319	259	210
Expressed as difference from lowest cost site	–	197	137	88

differences in journey cost of people who travel, whatever the site of the airport, and differences in journey to work costs (the latter were excluded in the final report).

Intangibles

The intangibles to be measured are time, noise and amenity.

Various forecasting and measurement problems that arose in the course of the analysis are described in Chapter 9; here the aim is to set out a presentation of the results that seem to us to be useful.

PRESENTATION OF COST BENEFIT ANALYSIS

The results of any economic analysis can, of course, be presented in a large number of different ways; the following suggestion is derived from experience of presenting economic data to management committees of various kinds. It seems to be appropriate for Government officials at various levels who, while wishing to retain a proper basis on which to exercise their judgement do not have the time or inclination to go into any great detail.

The written presentation is however only part of the problem. In many countries and particularly in the UK, decisions on problems of this kind are increasingly influenced by public opinion. This opinion is subject to a great many pressures and those who stand to gain from one solution or another are often prepared to spend very large sums of money on public relations campaigns. It is vital, therefore, that those responsible for analyses of this kind should ensure than an objective account of their study is given a fair hearing. In the author's experience this can only be done by devoting considerable resources to a series of verbal presentations of the work which has been carried out. Such presentations have a number of aims.

1　They ensure that the key points of the analysis are properly presented (for example, those in the summary document proposed in this chapter).

2　They enable questions and misunderstandings to be cleared up on the spot. In particular, if such presentations are properly timed, they can avoid for formation of ill-informed opposition.

3　A face-to-face confrontation with those responsible for carrying out the recommendations of the Roskill Commission pointed to a victory of common sense over the working of a faceless bureaucracy. It is extremely important in such an atmosphere for those responsible for the study to stand up and be counted.

The report would contain the following sections.

(a) A brief summary of the overall project.

(b) The main economic conclusions.

(c) The list of the most important assumptions that had to be made during the analysis.

(d) The key results of sensitivity analysis designed to see what will happen if some of these main assumptions were to be incorrect.

Table 8.1, giving more detail of the results of the analysis, would be attached as an appendix. The nature and scope of appendices to the main presentation does of course depend upon circumstances. In the case of the Roskill Commission

of course depend upon circumstances. In the case of the Roskill Commission total published evidence ran to several thousand pages; the object of this summary however, is to present the key results to someone who has not too much time in which to absorb them.

TABLE OF RESULTS

Table 8.1 gives the present value of the various terms in our expression of collective utility discounted to 1975 and expressed in £millions. In some cases, it might be preferable to give a year-by-year presentation and follow this by the discounted result; in this instance this would have been rather cumbersome in view of the four solutions that are being compared.

The following comments can be made about the way in which this has been drawn up.

1   The base for all the terms in Table 8.1 is to a certain extent arbitrary; in the Commission's final report the figures in each line represent differences from the site with the lowest cost for the item examined, for example, Cublington in the case of time.

2   The research team did not calculate the total profit of the various organizations concerned; for example, in the case of the BAA. the term concerned was limited to construction costs and the acquisition of land (the figures quoted in our table include a number of items that will not appear in the books of the BAA, and, in particular, the capital cost at Luton).

3   The profit generated by BR at the margin — that is, the difference between behavioural costs (the price paid by the passenger) and marginal resource costs — was not calculated by the Research Team and it was difficult to

derive exactly; the figures shown are therefore the author's estimate.

4   The major effects taken into account for the profitability of airlines, involve costs in the air.   Unfortunately it was not possible to take into account the costs of such things as the location and relocation of engineering facilities or the possibility of using common engineering facilities at one of the sites and not at others.

5   The economic effect on general business is almost entirely in terms of the time and cost to business executives due to differences in surface access.

6   The item 'removal costs' is included although no separate evaluation was made of all of it; it was included in the item 'cost of noise'.

The choice of the year to which discounting has been carried out is quite arbitrary.   Although it has no effect on the relative position of the four sites it does, however, influence the absolute size of any differences that might be found.

EXAMPLE BASED ON THE ROSKILL COMMISSION

The following is given as an example of the layout and content of the summary of a cost benefit exercise.   This would be appropriate in informing a top decision maker.

General description

It has been decided to build a Third London Airport to deal with the situation that will arise when the existing ones in the South East of England reach capacity in about 1980.   Preliminary analysis narrowed down the choice to four possible sites, Cublington, Thurleigh, Nuthampstead and Foulness.

The analysis was carried out from the viewpoint of the British community with one important exception; foreign business and leisure air travellers were treated in exactly the same way as British ones.   Such treatment of foreigners seems consistent with past British Government practice on such things as the National Health Service and also with current economic practice in the analysis of transport investments.

The results of the analysis were discussed with all the interested parties in the course of a series of public hearings; many of these parties submitted independent evidence which has been taken into account in the results now presented.

In accordance with present Treasury policy the analysis was carried out ignoring tax payments* and using a discount rate of 10 per cent for the evaluation of future cash flows.   It showed that there was a significant difference between Foulness and the inland sites in favour of the latter; Nuthampstead and Thurleigh were marginally less attractive than Cublington although the differences were less than the expected errors in the calculation.

---

* This could be equally well justified by the analysis put forward in Chapter 2.

Summary of economic analysis

Present value of costs and benefits

The present value of costs and benefits resulting from the analysis are as follows discounted to 1975 and expressed as differences from the lowest cost site Cublington.

		£m
Foulness		197
Nuthampstead		137
Thurleigh		88

Estimate of error*

The standard deviation of the estimates of costs and benefits at any one site is estimated at £23m; there is therefore only a 5 per cent probability of obtaining a difference between two sites greater than £50m due solely to random errors.

Total capital cost

The total capital cost of the airport will be between £500m and £600m undiscounted; the equivalent figures discounted to 1982 are £280m and £320m respectively.

Major assumptions

Traffic

The overall build-up of traffic in the total airport system covering Heathrow, Gatwick, the Third London Airport, Luton and Manchester will be as shown in Table 8.2.

		All Figures are in Millions		
Year	*Cublington*	*Foulness*	*Nuthampstead*	*Thurleigh*
1981	55	55	55	55
1991	117	114	116	117
2000	211	196	206	210

Table 8.2

Traffic at the Third London Airport itself will be as shown in Table 8.3.

Modal split

The modal split of passengers between road and rail varies slightly year by year and between airports; however, in all cases it is between 50 and 60 per cent by rail.

---

* The Research Team calculated an estimate of the error of their calculations: although it would be difficult to attach a precise statistical significance to this the idea is nevertheless an attractive one. The derivation of this error term is briefly discussed in Chapter 9.

All Figures are in Millions

	Cublington	Foulness	Nuthampstead	Thurleigh
1991				
Business	8	5	8	7
Leisure	28	19	26	28
Total	36	24	34	35
2000				
Business	18	14	18	16
Leisure	94	70	89	94
Total	112	84	107	110

Table 8.3

Value of time

It has been assumed that values of time are related to the salary level of the traveller. The values used for business and leisure travellers are as follows.

1 Leisure travellers would pay £0.30 an hour in order to save time on the surface and air legs of the journey.

2 Businesses would be prepared to pay £2.60 an hour in order to shorten the journey time of their employees.

Furthermore, it is assumed that all time spent travelling, either in the aircraft or on the ground to and from the airport, is of no value for business purposes.

Foreigners

It has been assumed that foreigners attach similar values to losses of their time as those applicable to British passengers; thus, these losses have been taken into the calculation in exactly the same way as for British passengers.

Noise

Households exposed to noise were assumed either to move and to bear the removal costs, loss of consumer surplus and depreciation on their house or else to stay and suffer the nuisance. Furthermore, noise values varied according to the market price of the house concerned. The average cost to each household that emerged from these calculations were as given in Table 8.4.

NNI	Total noise cost per house (£)
Greater than 55	530
45 – 55	440
35 – 45	220

Table 8.4

The figures at Cublington and Nuthampstead were somewhat higher than these averages and those at Foulness and Thurleigh rather lower.

British Rail

British Rail was assumed to make a considerable profit at the margin; the marginal cost per hundred passenger miles is only £0.20 whereas the average fare is £2.

The difference in profit of the BAA at the various sites was assumed to be entirely because of the difference in capital costs (adjusted to bring all four sites onto the same volume basis); no further difference in profit was thought likely.

Defence costs

The defence costs shown in Table 8.1 given in the appendix were the subject of discussion and cross-examination *in camera.*

Luton

If one of the inland sites were to be chosen it would be necessary to close down Luton Airport for operational or economic reasons. However, if Foulness were to be chosen Luton would be left open. An evaluation has been carried out which shows that the solution of using Foulness alone would be less attractive on cost benefit grounds than Foulness plus Luton.

Sensitivity analysis

The two causes of difference between the four sites that involve the greatest uncertainty are: (1) the cost of time; and (2) the cost of noise.

The evaluation was therefore repeated using different values of these two factors and this gave the results in Table 8.5.

It should be noted that in no case is Cublington less than £66m better than all the other sites. The difference between Cublington and Foulness is never less than £151m.

CONCLUSION

The presentation in Table 8.5 represents a logical way of setting out the results of a cost benefit analysis. The actual length of the document, the quantity and nature of the appendices and the degree of sensitivity analysis produced will of course vary with the circumstances, and in particular the size of the sums of money involved. The essential points are as follows.

1   The results are clearly stated.

2   The main assumptions on which they depend are also clearly set out.

3   Sufficient sensitivity analysis is carried out to give the answer to all the most probably 'what would happen if ....?' questions. This sensitivity analysis is designed to give a measure of the risk attaching to the project and is the essential raw material upon which the decision-maker can exercise his judgement.

Aggregates of Inter-site Differences
on Alternative Time and Noise Values (£m discounted to 1982)

| | High time values | | | Low time values | | |
| | Noise values | | | Noise values | | |
	High	Middle	Low	High	Middle	Low
Foulness – Nuthampstead	32	60	75	–	28	43
Foulness – Thurleigh	106	109	109	85	88	88
Foulness – Cublington	192	197	199	151	156	158
Nuthampstead – Thurleigh	74	49	34	85	60	45
Nuthampstead – Cublington	160	137	124	151	128	115
Thurleigh – Cublington	86	88	90	66	68	70

The values used in calculating this table are:

Time: high – business £2.60 leisure £0.30
         low – business £1.50 leisure £0.10

Noise: high – middle +30%
         low – middle −30%

Table 8.5

Some of the problems raised by this analysis of the Third London Airport are discussed in Chapter 9.

9

The Third London Airport

BACKGROUND AND GENERAL APPROACH

The analysis carried out and the background to it were summed up in Chapter 8. In this the figures were presented in the layout developed in Chapter 2. In fact the Research Team used a far more general framework of reasoning in which terms were dealt with 'on their merits'. While there are many possible acceptable ways of presenting the same analysis, this lack of a specific theoretical framework derived step by step made discussion difficult at some points. The most striking example was the case for the inclusion or exclusion of the profits of the British Airports Authority and this is discussed on page 116.

In addition to the question of profit the three theoretical points that caused the most interest were: the problem of weighting (discussed in Chapter 7); the inclusion of foreigners; and the question of marginality. This latter point had been raised by the Research Team in their treatment of passenger user costs but also raised in connection with the effect of noise on householders.

WEIGHTING

The problem of weighting arose most acutely when comparing the cost of noise and the benefits to passengers of reduced journey times. Specifically the choice of Foulness rather than an inland site was felt to cause less nuisance to people on the ground whereas it was rendered uneconomic in the cost benefit analysis by the very high cost to passengers. Arguments in favour of 'rectifying' this situation were based on the following ideas.

Equity

The average salary of air travellers is considerably above the national mean. There was considerable discussion about what the actual figures should be but the Research Team in Volume 7 quoted £3100 which should be compared with the national average of about £1300.

It was suggested that all time savings should be reduced by statistically diminishing the air travellers' salaries to the national mean. This meant reducing the total time cost by a factor of about 2. In discussion it was pointed out that this treatment could only be applied to leisure time. The whole notion of distribution of income and possible corrections for it refers to consumers; in the case of business profits, which are affected by losses of business time, no convincing argument was put forward for weighting.

The counter argument is the one set out in Chapter 7; this is that society has for a variety of reasons accepted the existing unequal distribution of income. The assumption that the state would prefer everyone to earn the same amount, which underlay this particular weighting argument, therefore seems unlikely.

The reason why society is prepared to accept inequalities of income is that these are necessary in order to preserve some incentive for people to work harder, to be successful, to qualify in exacting professions, and so on. Of course if all individual incomes should be examined one by one, a whole variety of adjustments would be desirable; the point is that no way can be seen of economically effecting such a redistribution without having damaging effects on the economy as a whole.

The fact that society attaches more importance to the satisfaction of those citizens who contribute most to it can be quite strikingly illustrated by an example put forward by one witness during the hearings. He remarked that society obviously attached an equal value to the satisfaction produced by a poor man's pint of beer and to that produced by a rich man's pint. Although this is a very appealing idea at first sight it is clearly not true; consider the effect when prices are raised. At some point the poor man will stop drinking beer because he can no longer afford it, whereas the rich man will continue to do so.

Once society has accepted inequality of income, and, in particular, once it has allowed more responsible or hard working citizens to retain a greater reward for their labours than those whose contribution is smaller, it has automatically given them greater economic weight and the means to express their wishes. In a military context society clearly attaches more value to the life and comfort of a general than to that of a private soldier. Equally the value of a prime minister is higher still. The loss to the community if a general is tired because he has had to pass the night out of doors in pouring rain is more than the loss that would be expected if an ordinary soldier were exposed to the same conditions.

In the terms used in Chapter 2, even if the satisfaction subjectively felt by two individuals is identical, society does not usually attach equal weight to their satisfaction when building up its collective utility function. The greater importance of one rather than another is commonly expressed by allowing him more money; this money is available to procure such advantages as a shorter journey to an airport and this does not call for any correction in the form of weighting.

The incidence of taxation

A second argument was that society taxes people at different income levels using different rates. For example, it could be that someone earning £600 a year would pay no tax at all whereas a person earning £10 000 might pay 50 per cent. This is clear evidence that society does not wish the more highly paid person to benefit fully from the value placed on his work by the economy, that is, his employer. It was then suggested that in such circumstances the values quoted by the well-paid person should be reduced by a half; in particular if he were willing to pay £1 an hour to avoid additional travelling time, the overall cost benefit analysis should include only 50 per cent of this.

However, this argument is demonstrably false, as it would amount to society correcting for the same thing twice. The fact that the community does not wish him to retain the full £10 000, and removes half of it by way of tax, does not mean that it would wish to reduce the balance by a further 50 per cent. In other words, the community accepts the distribution of income after tax whereas it is recognized that the situation before tax is in need of correction. (Tax refers not only to income taxes but to all other forms of allowances and subsidies.)

Common sense

A further argument was that the relative sizes of the two terms representing noise and time offended against common sense. Arguments such as this should not be rejected out of hand, as they often reflect the expert's deeper knowledge of a subject. They are rather similar to the marketing director's reaction referred to in Chapter 1; although he can find no flaw in the market research or in the reasoning that has been used, his experience tells him that the rate of growth included in an investment proposal is just not possible.

This, however, by no means indicates that such opinions are always right, and in the present case the argument had little value. The fact that passenger user costs should dominate the calculation is hardly surprising in view of the fact that we are considering a transport investment. The fact that noise nuisance is so low merely means that all the sites on the short list had been carefully chosen.

General amenity undervalued

Several parties felt that the loss of general amenity had been undervalued; they suggested that this could be corrected for by some form of weighting. This was a confusion of terms as the object of weighting is not to correct errors in estimation but to deal with the rather more technical points of the distribution of income. To take a case in point; if the value of a series of country houses had been underestimated, the solution is to revise the estimate rather than to introduce a highly dubious multiplication factor at some later stage.

The whole object of the analysis is to make it easy to identify assumptions that have been made and to put these forward for discussion. This is only possible if the case is set out in a clear straightforward way and if the working is unobscured by the introduction of a variety of unidentified correction factors. The situation is rather similar to the business context in which a number of people are allowed to introduce 'reserves' or provisions for contingencies into a calculation. This generally results in someone further up the chain automatically recorrecting the estimates; the final figures are then no longer identifiable with anything concrete and it is extremely difficult to assess them.

Marginal and structural change

A further argument used in favour of weighting was the notion of marginality. This was raised in two separate ways, both of which took as their starting point the economic theory known as the diminishing marginal utility of income. This theory, which is supported by very little factual evidence, but which does not seem unreasonable on general behavioural grounds, states that the satisfaction produced by the expenditure of £1 decreases as income rises. In other words a rich man would probably have to spend £100 to obtain the same additional satisfaction as could be got by a poor man for £10.

Figure 9.1 shows this graphically. It shows that a certain amount of expenditure is required before a person can live at all; beyond this point satisfaction rises very rapidly with expenditure as the individual is able to afford some form of shelter, clothing, and so on; it then gradually falls off as expenditure becomes concentrated on luxuries. Suppose a person is at point A with income and expenditure equal to I and satisfaction S. The satisfaction that he would obtain from a small (marginal) increase or decrease in expenditure is represented by the slope of the line CAF.

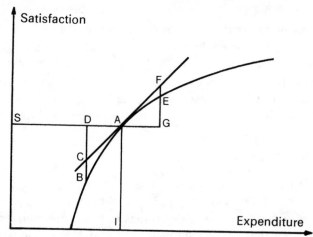

Figure 9.1   *Satisfaction produced by expenditure decreases as income rises*

In particular if his satisfaction increased and decreased in exact proportion to his expenditure an increase in income from A to G would produce the increase in satisfaction GF and a decrease from A to D would reduce his satisfaction by DC. In fact, as can be seen from the graph, the actual increase in satisfaction is not FG but the smaller amount EG. Similarly the loss of satisfaction is not DC but the rather greater amount DB.

In the case of the Third London Airport, the only two groups of people likely to be affected in a way that was not marginal were the travellers already referred to (and who are looked at again on page 115) and the owners of houses. Some of this latter group would be losing about £500 in the form of reduced house values, and so on, and it was argued that this sum was large enough for the effect that we have described to be noticeable; thus although house prices might fall by £500 the subjective loss to those involved would be greater and the remedy would be to increase the loss by a form of 'weighting'.

Once again we are involved in a problem of language; however, in the framework that has been developed in this book the term 'weighting' would be reserved for items connected with the income effect; a better treatment of the fact that house owners might be subject to structural rather than marginal changes, would be to deal with them in the way that is described for passengers' time (*see* page 115). The term structural is used in opposition to marginal; it refers to changes which produce an effect on individuals that introduces the notion of diminishing marginal utility of income or an effect on goods or services which moves them some way along their demand curve. In both cases the essential notion is that the simple linearity assumption, that satisfaction is proportional to expenditure or that demand is proportional to price, is no longer valid.

The following points were raised during the discussion of this aspect of weighting.

1   That £500 is marginal for a change in housing costs. It was argued that this sum represented about 10 per cent of the total cost of accommo-dation, and that expenditure on such accommodation was about 15 per cent of a family's total income. Thus the change would only influence income by about 2 per cent and this could be thought of as marginal.

2   For some people housing is in a quite exceptional category in that they consent to considerable sacrifices in order to amass the fairly small sum required for a deposit on a house; a fall in price of only a few per cent is therefore greatly magnified in terms of their own personal capital, the possibility of obtaining another house, and so on.

3   The problem would disappear if adequate compensation were to be paid; this would move the individual's income and satisfaction back from point B on the curve to point A (*Figure 9.1*).

Treatment of foreigners

One of the results of the lack of a very clear theoretical framework was that the Research Team was not obliged to make any very firm statement on the viewpoint of its investigation. As has been seen, the composition of collective utility is very different according to the community that is being considered, and in particular according to whether a national or an international viewpoint is being taken. It was agreed that in principle the Third London Airport should be regarded from the point of view of the citizens of the UK; however, this gave rise to problems concerning the following terms.

1   Savings of time and other costs by foreign leisure travellers.

2   Savings in costs by travellers employed by firms owned by foreigners; it should be noted that there is a fairly material difference between the firms whose business is outside the UK and those located within the country. In the latter case approximately half of any change in profit would be paid over to the UK community by way of taxation.

3   The profits of foreign airlines.

There was fairly general agreement that in the context of a major transport investment an exception should be made to the normal procedure; the losses and gains just referred to should be treated in exactly the same way as if they had been incurred by British firms and individuals.

The most convincing argument in favour of this treatment was based on the idea that international cooperation pays off. If there were only two nations involved, and if each were to make an airport location decision based on the interests of its own nationals, both could be uneconomic when looked at from the point of view of the community made up of the two nations. Expressed in another way, it would be wrong to discriminate against foreigners in an essentially international situation, as this would provoke similar discrimination against one's own nationals in the future. Further evidence that was quoted was the attitude of the British Government towards the National Health Service in permitting it to be used by foreigners. Here it was stated that the reasoning for having such a policy was that similar facilities would be made available to British nationals abroad, and that such international reciprocity was in everyone's interest.

However, as in many questions raised by cost benefit analysis, the final decision was essentially one of judgement. It could well be that in a more nationalistic situation, the opposite treatment would have been adopted, that is the exclusion of all benefits concerning foreigners.

MARGINALITY

The effect of marginal changes on individuals were referred to when discussing weighting and the effect of noise. However, a further point on which the Research Team quite properly moved away from the marginality assumption concerned passenger-user costs. The situation is shown in *Figure 9.2*.

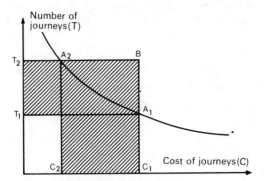

Figure 9.2   *Cost and number of journeys*

We are comparing two situations, A_1 and A_2. At A_1 the cost of each journey is C_1 and T_1 passengers travel; this could be the situation at Foulness. A second solution is now examined, for example, Cublington, for which the cost of travel is lower (C_2); this encourages more people to travel and the total number of journeys is T_2. The analysis developed for marginal changes would suggest that the net benefit from moving from Foulness to Cublington would be equal to the sum of three terms.

1 The consumption of additional journeys evaluated at the market price:

$$C_1 (T_2 - T_1)$$

2 The savings of existing passengers (this is a case of unwanted consumption in reverse):

$$T_1 (C_1 - C_2)$$

3 Less the additional resource costs used is

$$(T_2 R_2 - T_1 R_1)$$

(The difference between R_1 and R_2 is caused solely by different quantities of various resources used, as all costs are calculated at constant prices.)

The sum of the first two expressions is shown by the shaded area in *Figure 9.2*.

This is only justified, however, providing the area of the triangle A_2A_1B is sufficiently small. In a marginal transformation this is so, as the triangle is a second order term: the product of ΔT and ΔC which are each already small. However, if the change in price were sufficiently large for this area to be no longer negligible, it would be necessary to adopt the slightly more sophisticated techniques mentioned in Chapter 2 and calculate not T_2BA_1T but T_2A_2 A_1T_1. The justification of this is that whereas the first few additional passengers over T_1 valued their journey at almost C_1, this valuation subsequently declined and the last few only valued theirs at C_2.

It is thus clear that the total valuation of the additional journeys is the area $T_2A_2A_1T_1$, just referred to, less the change in resource costs.

If the company providing the transport were to be one of those whose management was optimal (*see* Chapter 4), we can say that its profit is the same in each case expressed in constant prices.

Thus :
$$T_1 (C_1 - R_1) = T_2 (C_1 - R_2)$$

Rearranging this equation

$$C_1 (T_2 - T_1) = T_2R_2 - T_1R_1$$

This simply states that the value of the additional journeys is equal to the resource costs employed in making them possible. This means that the traditional treatment would eliminate (1) from (3) altogether and that the expression for passenger user costs would be reduced to $T_1 (C_1 - C_2)$, that is, the saving on the existing journeys.

The Research Team used the rather more sophisticated approach and assumed that A_1A_2 is a straight line; this meant that they subtracted the area of the triangle A_1A_2B from the terms just discussed and ended up with the expression:

$$T_1 (C_1 - C_2) + \tfrac{1}{2} (T_2 - T_1) (C_1 - C_2)$$

BUSINESS PROFITS

The Research Team had based its treatment on a frame of reference which did not include business profits; in the event this was not wholly satisfactory and this was particularly noticeable in the treatment of the profits of the BAA. However, it also enabled some quite important assumptions on the profitability of other undertakings to go almost unnoticed; the most striking case concerns BR.

The British Airports Authority

The Research Team considered that it was only necessary to make forecasts of one item in the profit and loss account of the BAA; this was the capital cost of building the airport. This treatment raised the following points.

1   The assumption that all other items would net out is very similar to our own statement that business is managed optimally. It was expressed by saying[1]: 'The present analysis does not attempt to estimate transfer payments taking the form of what economists call 'Producer's surplus' – that is, any transitory abnormal profit element in the costs of goods and services used. To ignore the presence of producers' surplus is tantamount to assuming that no more than reasonably competitive conditions in the supplying industry which is probably not far from the truth.' In the case of the BAA this assumption was, however, rather unrealistic; in the final report it was recognized that the inclusion of this item would be justified theoretically; a figure of £30m was quoted.

2   The selection of one term or group of terms and the assumption that the net effect on all others will be zero is perfectly reasonable. The absolute figures in cost benefit analysis are usually of very little significance for this reason; the base line or starting point is extremely arbitrary. This situation is also common in normal industrial evaluations, where one only looks at those items affected by an investment, and does not attempt to recalculate the whole of the company's profits.

3   The Research Team quite properly recognized that they could not make any direct comparisons between capital costs based on different traffic volumes; these have first to be adjusted to bring them on to the same basis. Traffic volumes are, of course, automatically adjusted for in a fuller profit calculation, as a larger more expensive site receives greater benefits in terms of sales.

In the present case this adjustment was in two parts: first, the capital costs of Foulness (the only significant traffic differences were between Foulness and the level estimated for the three inland sites) were re-calculated on the basis of the inland site traffic levels minus Luton. Second, the capital cost of extending Luton to deal with the traffic that will pass through it, was added to the cost of the Foulness solution.

The BAA not surprisingly, carried out a much fuller investigation into their profit position; this showed that there were substantial differences in profit on other items between the four sites amounting to some £70m in net present value (discounted to 1975). Two points are worth noting about this calculation.

(a) It was carried out in constant prices; this is, of course, not necess-
     arily the way in which the Authority would calculate its profits for
     its own internal purposes; it is, however, essential for comparability
     with an overall evaluation of the cost benefit type.

(b) The calculations were carried out before tax.

Both these items are discussed on page 30 and in the conclusion in Chapter
14.

An interesting practical point was that the Authority thought it worth while to
set up a computerized model of its operations; this made it possible to rapidly
recalculate its overall profit position to take into account a wide range of
differing parameters and in particular different traffic assumptions. This
situation was highly desirable, as results were needed during the hearings of the
Commission, and this amounted to an almost 'on line' situation.

British Rail

The profits of BR did not appear as a term in the Research Team's evaluation.
However, the method of calculation was equivalent to assuming that there would
be very large differences; this was because two different costs of rail transport
were used at different stages in the argument.

1   When looking at behavioural cost for such things as modal split, access-
     ibility, and so on, a fare of about £2 per 100 miles was employed.

2   For the evaluation of passenger user cost the Team used the resource cost
     of rail transport which was assumed to be as low as £0.20 per 100 miles.
     The resulting figures did not represent, therefore, the actual cost to the
     passenger, but rather the expense incurred by BR in carrying him. The
     person using the railway would have paid out not only the sums that
     were attributed to him, but also an additional amount represented by the
     profit of BR. The presentation in Table 8.1 shows the 'true' passenger
     user costs, that is, the amount paid by the passenger; it then deducts, as a
     separate item, the profit of the railway. The end result is clearly the same
     in both cases.
         The advantage of showing profit specifically in a case like this, is to
     draw attention in a rather more graphic manner to the profits of the
     company concerned. In the present case a rough estimate showed that
     the calculation had effectively supposed that the profit made by BR on
     the additional mileage in getting to Foulness (this is essentially mileage on
     main line track) would amount to some £60m in present value terms.
     This item, which is the second largest difference in the entire calculation,
     received only a very limited discussion and this was, to some extent,
     because its importance had never been identified.

10

The Channel Tunnel

INTRODUCTION

In this chapter we will describe a series of studies designed to evaluate the construction of a tunnel under the English channel. These were carried out by British and French consultants, and covered the period from April 1971 until June 1973[17]. The clients for these studies were the two companies concerned with promoting this transport investment. The initial study was concerned, only with the economic justification of the venture, as such.

The UK Department of the Environment then decided to ask the British consultants to produce a limited cost benefit analysis; this was to take into account the effects on other organizations within the UK and on passengers. The organizations included shipping companies, airlines, railways, ports and road operators[18]. Other wider cost benefit studies were carried out internally but were not published.

THE ALTERNATIVES

The basic alternatives considered by these studies were the construction of the tunnel and its associated railway investment on the one hand, and an expansion of existing shipping and port facilities on the other. (This alternative was only explicit in the case of the cost benefit study.) These alternatives will first be described; we will then go on to discuss briefly a number of others, some of which were included in the studies by way of sensitivity analysis.

The tunnel

At an early stage it was decided that the tunnel should provide for rail-borne traffic only (including cars and lorries on a roll on/roll off basis). Considerations which led to this decision included the problems of ventilation, the consequences of accidents, vehicles running out of petrol, and so on, in a tunnel 30 miles long. and the capacity which could be obtained from various forms of operation. The double track rail facility would run from Cheriton near Folkestone to Sangatte near Calais. It would be shared by the shuttle trains between terminal stations close to the end of the tunnel, and mainline long distance trains bringing passengers and through freight traffic.

The plans examined in the study assumed that the journey time from Paris to London would be 3 hours 45 minutes and that from London to Brussels slightly shorter.

The basic service would be hourly supplemented by additional services at peak times. A night sleeper service would also be provided to more distant destinations and it was envisaged that special charter trains would cater for inclusive tour holiday-makers.

In addition to transporting lorries freight services would be split between special trains for bulk commodities, and freight liners providing a direct, through rail service for containers between specially constructed terminals.

The ferry trains provided by the tunnel operating authority would be composed either of double-deck wagons carrying 260 cars or else single-deck wagons taking lorries and coaches as well as cars. Road vehicles would be driven on and off the ferry trains by their own drivers, and the overall time from entry at one terminal to exit from the other has been estimated at 1 hour.

In addition to the tunnel, there would continue to be fairly substantial shipping services across the Channel. As will be seen from the traffic forecasts, the reduction in the level of traffic resulting from the construction of the tunnel varies considerably according to the sea route.

The prices charged by existing ferries appeared to be excessively high in comparison with other services over similar distances, for example, Malmo — Copenhagen. This led to a very interesting study of the likely reactions of ferry owners in reducing prices to compete more effectively with the tunnel. Although the study confirmed that 'for modern vessels, the profit rates on the Dover Straits routes are high at the present level of fares', it emerged that the scope for reduction was less than appeared at first sight. This was essentially because of the very high peaking on the Dover Straits routes. Nevertheless, an iterative process was carried out with the aim of arriving at a stable pricing situation under all of the following conditions.

1   Ferries were operating under conditions such that the rate of return on capital was equal to a predetermined minimum yield.

2   Neither the tunnel nor the ferries could increase their revenue by changing their tariffs.

3   All potential demand was carried by one means or another.

No tunnel situation

If the tunnel were not to be built, it was assumed that the vast majority of freight and accompanied cars traffic would use modern ferries, that is, vessels with a capacity of about 360 cars. Even larger ships were also examined. It was felt that hovercraft services did not appear to offer a satisfactory alternative to ferries; operating costs are considerably higher per capacity mile and present services operate either at a loss, or at best are only marginally profitable. The Department of Trade and Industry were consulted on the possibility of technological advance; their view was that there was little potential for further development in the light of their present knowledge. Prospects for hydrofoils appeared even less promising than for hovercraft.

In the absence of the tunnel, passengers travelling without cars for both pleasure and business, would revert to the ferries and also to air transport.

Other possibilities

Two rail schemes were examined by British Railways and the Department of the Environment. The first, high investment strategy, involved building new lines from London to the tunnel terminal at a cost of £101m (discounted). The second low investment strategy, would cost approximately £20m a saving in capital costs of approximately £81m. However, it would make the journey about 30 minutes longer for both passengers from or through London. Furthermore, British Railways claimed that there would be a severe shortage of capacity in the peak period if no new line were constructed, and that the total demand that could be carried under the low investment rail strategy would be severely restricted. The consultants assumed that this would result in the total traffic diverted from air services to the tunnel being only half as great as with the high investment strategy. They noted that this would have little effect on the rate of return of the tunnel, but that 'before any decision was taken to proceed with the low rail investment policy, it would be necessary to carry out a detailed investigation'. It is interesting to notice that this quotation is taken from the document *The Channel Tunnel: A United Kingdom Transport Cost Benefit Study*[18] whereas the justification for the high investment rail strategy is extremely sketchy and is entirely in terms of the profit earned by the private investors in the tunnel. The omissions in the analysis are discussed on page 133.

A second alternative concerns the carriage of freight. The intensive use of the channel ports for freight shipment to the continent is the result of private decisions taken by industrialists, shippers, and so on. These take into account the costs to them but not the impact on the community of road construction, noise, and so on. In may be that in the context of such a major investment in transport to the continent, alternative routes for freight should have been studied. In particular it could be in the community's interest to ensure that freight from the Midlands or the North of England uses East coast rather than channel ports, and that a large fixed investment perpetuating the present pattern should have some costs set against it in this respect*.

The treatment of hovercraft also seems surprising. The present generation of hovercraft is to some extent in the prototype stage. It seems strange that operating costs will show no reduction over the study period†.

A final development which would have a substantial influence on the outcome of the decision would arise if holidaymakers with cars were to change their behaviour substantially. By this we are referring to the use of fly/drive and other similar schemes by which passengers travel using conventional means of transport, and then hire cars at their destination. This could be a particularly important point in the context of the tunnel as over half of its revenue will come from such passengers. The problems that this raises will be discussed when we turn to the forecasting methods which were used.

FORECASTING

As usual, the forecasting of traffic that would use the tunnel was split into three stages.

1 Obtaining an up-to-date picture of the existing situation. This involved the mounting of a number of surveys to cover the different kinds of traffic for both passengers and freight.

2 A forecasting exercise to obtain total traffic that could conceivably use the tunnel.

3 A traffic allocation exercise to determine the share which would in fact use the tunnel.

Although the traffic forecasting exercise was an extremely painstaking analysis of the various factors affecting traffic generation it was essentially a statistical extrapolation. It was found that the number of holidays taken abroad could be corollated with family income, the number of persons in the household, the social class of the person concerned, the cost of a holiday, the age of the youngest child and so forth. This total was then broken down into passengers by car, charter/package or those travelling independently using similar relationships.

---

* These questions may have been raised by the Department of the Environment in unpublished studies.

† This assumption of no material change was made by the Department of Trade and Industry.

The adequacy of procedures of this kind depends upon the kind of investment which will be based on them. In the author's view it is unfortunate that so little creative long-term forecasting has been carried out, particularly when dealing with projects the size of the Channel tunnel. In addition to the examples quoted in Chapter 4, a recent exercise using prospective methods is the one commissioned by Paris airport in the context of long-term studies on a fourth airport for Paris (that is, in addition to Charles de Gaulle). In the context of the present study, a particularly important point which might have been explored concerns the exact pattern of holiday traffic using cars. The use of the family's own car is clearly conditioned by a very wide range of factors such as the following.

(a) Car ownership.

(b) Relative costs of taking one's own car and hiring.

(c) Effects of congestion in holiday areas.

(d) General acceptability of car renting as such.

Some factors of this kind can be quantified and properly introduced into statistical forecasting models. However, others need more creative forecasting techniques. Clients commissioning studies and consultants carrying them out nevertheless tend to stick to purely numerical methods; these have a great appeal in that statistical analysis can be carried out on them, 'confidence' limits set, and so on. However, in long-term studies they can be very misleading.

Most of the remarks in this section apply to the forecasting of passenger traffic, and the overall results are summarized in Table 10.1.

Tunnel Traffic Central Growth Assumption 1990

	Millions of crossings via the tunnel	Percentage via the tunnel
Passengers without vehicles		
Holiday makers	11.9	23
Business	3.1	12
Total	15	19
Passengers with vehicles		
Holiday makers	13.2	72
Business	1.4	76
Total	14.5	72
Overall total	29.5	30

Table 10.1

Alternative forecasts were prepared on different growth assumption and in particular a lower rate of increase of gross national product. The latter led to a total forecast of 24.2 million passengers that is a reduction of 18 per cent. The reductions were spread more or less proportionately across all the main categories of traffic.

The freight traffic was forecast using similar procedures, and it was estimated to be as shown in Table 10.2 in 1990.

	Millions of tons
Through trains	5.2
Roll on/roll off	2.7
Total	7.9

Table 10.2

EVALUATION FROM THE COMPANY'S POINT OF VIEW

As we noted in the introduction, the initial evaluation of the effects of the tunnel was carried out from the point of view of the company owning it. We noted in Chapter 6 that most cost benefit evaluations are carried out in constant money, that is, excluding the effects of general inflation. However, when looking at the position of a company, particularly if there are unindexed borrowings, it is usual to work in current money. Differences can be very important when inflation rates are high and this has given rise to the current debate in the UK and elsewhere over inflation-free accounting. The basic idea here is that ordinary accounts should be expressed in constant money to eliminate stock profits due to inflation and to ensure that adequate provision is made for depreciation. On the money market, similar ideas are expressed in terms of indexed loans.

The basic cost of constructing the tunnel including interest during the construction period, financing costs and inflation, was as shown in Table 10.3.

	£m
Construction costs at January 1973 prices	468
Interest	192
Inflation	186
Total	846

Table 10.3

A little over half of the figure of £468m is accounted for by the construction of the tunnel itself; £80m is the cost of terminals and the balance covers rolling stock, project development, engineering and contingencies. This cost is phased over the construction period from 1973 to 1980 with most activity in the years 1976, 1977 and 1978.

The revenue forecasts for 1981 and 1990 in the two growth assumptions were as shown in Table 10.4 (expressed in money values including inflation).

	1981 (£m)	*1990 (£m)*
Low growth assumption		
Passengers without vehicles	38	84
Passengers with vehicles	56	156
Freight	18	46
Total	112	286
Central growth assumption		
Passengers without vehicles	42	98
Passengers with vehicles	64	211
Freight	22	64
Total	128	373

Table 10.4

In both series of figures, it is important to note that more than half of the income of the tunnel will come from passengers with vehicles. For this reason the forecasting of such traffic becomes particularly critical; if statistical methods turned out to be grossly unreliable due to the kind of factors which we mention in the previous section, this could put the tunnel's future in some doubt.

Estimates of operating costs covered the maintenance of the fixed installations and the costs of running the shuttle services and the terminals. A formula was produced which indicated operating costs of £16.6m in the first complete year of operation (1981), and £40m in 1990.

The consultants were asked to assume that 10 per cent of the total cost of £846m would be financed by risk capital, and the balance by loans. The average costs of these loans was assumed to be about 9 per cent with slightly lower rates on international and French loans and a higher one on British loans. The split is given in Table 10.5 and the final profitability calculations can be illustrated in Table 10.6.

The consultants used the operating profits generated year by year to calculate the internal rate of return for the project. This is the rate which was described in the example on page 83, that is, the rate at which the present value of all the

	Percentage
International market	25
British market	37.5
French market	37.5
Total	100

Table 10.5

cash flows connected with the project, including construction and operating receipts, is zero. The result was that on the central growth assumption, the internal rate of return over a 50-year period was 17 per cent. A number of points are worth noting about this rate of return.

1   When a project is financed, partly by borrowing and partly out of the investors own resources, there are two bases on which to calculate the rate. The first is the one which was used by the consultants; this takes the operating profit before debt service and the total construction costs. It is the economic yield for the entire project. A second possible definition, which would perhaps have been of more interest to the channel tunnel shareholders, would be based on the capital which they put into the venture, and the receipts which they obtain from it in the form of dividends. This was the calculation shown in the company prospectus for the placing of shares.

2   A great deal of confusion often arises over the inclusion or exclusion of tax. Normally this has the effect of dividing or multiplying the results by two. In the published summary, calculations were carried out before tax. As we have seen this is a correct approach when looking at the economics of the community. However, it is somewhat unreal when looking at the situation of a company.

3   We have already referred to the inclusion or exclusion of inflation. The consultants recognized that their initial yield calculations would give very high figures as the basic amounts discounted included inflation. They therefore deducted the retail price index inflation rate, to express the internal rate of return in real values. In the calculation of a return from the community's point of view, this treatment would be correct; however, it could be misleading when calculating from the company's point of view; this is because the cost of borrowing is a fixed item in monetary terms, and the application of inflation rates to it would lead to an under-estimation of the final yield to the shareholder.

This latter point will be illustrated in the following section when we refer to the analysis from the point of view of the community.

Profitability

	Low growth		Central growth	
	1981 *(£m)*	*1990* *(£m)*	*1981* *(£m)*	*1990* *(£m)*
Gross revenue	112	286	128	373
Operating costs	17	34	17	40
Operating profit	95	252	111	333
Debt service	69	89	69	89
Net receipts	26	163	42	244

Table 10.6

The consultants quite properly concluded their analysis from the company's point of view by carrying out a wide variety of sensitivity analyses. We have underlined the importance of such analyses throughout this book.

COST BENEFIT ANALYSIS[18]

In view of the very high degree of public participation in the financing of the project, and its potential effects on the community in other ways, it was felt necessary to enlarge the scope of the work carried out for the Channel Tunnel companies. The Department of the Environment therefore commissioned a study which has since been described as the cost benefit report. However, compared to the other studies examined in this book, this was essentially a limited exercise. The Department directed that the consultants should confine their attention to transport costs and benefits; other potential costs and benefits arising from the environmental impact of the tunnel and its effect on regional employment, and so on, were specifically excluded. In view of the course of public debate on the subject and the potential importance of some of the environmental nuisances, this limitation in the scope of the published documentation seems in retrospect unfortunate.

The costs and benefits which were finally quantified were as follows.

1 Economic effects on organizations.

   The tunnel operators
   Shipping companies
   Airlines

Railways
Port authorities
Road freight operators
Companies whose executives travel
Companies shipping freight

2 Economic effects on individuals: cost savings by leisure passengers.

3 Intangibles. The only intangible evaluated was the cost of time to leisure
   passengers.

For all of the aforementioned items, the consultants were only concerned with
that part involving UK interests. In the case of organizations this meant those
which belonged to UK owners. In the case of individuals, they were only dealing
with UK passengers. From a theoretical point of view, this approach is perfectly
proper although it could give rise to some rather anomalous conclusions if the
proportion of British passengers using the system were to be very different from
the proportion of British companies providing the services, and in particular the
British share in the tunnel. The results of this analysis are given in Table 10.7
which sums up the advantages flowing from the construction of the tunnel;
figures in brackets represent disadvantages.

Tunnel profits

All the figures in Table 10.7 are in real money, that is, excluding the effects of
inflation. Furthermore, they only relate to half the total venture, that is, the
proportion to be owned by British interests. For these reasons it is difficult to
reconcile them with the totals quoted earlier in the analysis from the company's
point of view. We would like to point out one important difference in basis,
however, this refers to the use of loan capital in a period of inflation.

The results of the sensitivity analysis on a lower growth assumption underline
the essential characteristics of the Channel tunnel; it is a very high fixed
investment whose profitability is critically dependent upon the volume of traffic
which it attracts. A reduction in revenue of 23.5 per cent (the difference between
the central and low growth assumptions in 1990) would halve the tunnel profit
whereas its effect on the profitability of other organizations would be much more
nearly in proportion to this loss of traffic.

Shipping

If the tunnel is built, shipping operators will make less profit than would
otherwise have been the case. This could arise for a number of reasons.

(a)   As we saw on page 120 the introduction of the tunnel is assumed to lead
       to a reduction in shipping prices. The calculation carried out by the

Growth Assumptions

	Central growth assumptions	Low growth assumptions
Economic effects on organizations		
Tunnel	228.4	118.4
Shipping lines	(68.2)	(40.6)
Airlines	(59.6)	(45.0)
Railways	10.4	(20.3)
Ports	3.0	(0.1)
Road freight operators	—	—
Road construction	6.9	6.9
Business travellers	36.8	29.3
Freight shippers	36.1	26.2
TOTAL	193.8	73.5
Cost and time effects on leisure passengers	98.0	74.4
TOTAL	291.8	147.9

Table 10.7

consultants takes this into account. In Chapter 2, page 17, we discussed the treatment of price in the calculation of profit and came to the conclusion that the underlying economic case was most clearly presented if the same price system was used in each alternative. This problem does underline the difficulty of treating terms in isolation, however, in the present analysis the overall treatment is correct as an adjustment is later made the effect of which is equal and opposite to that of a reduction in price. This adjustment calculates the savings made by passengers as a result of the price reduction.

(b) The disposal of surplus ships when the tunnel is opened. The assumption was made that these ships would have an alternative use value equal to only one-quarter of their replacement cost.

(c) A reduction in total volume of activity.

Airlines

The implication of the treatment adopted is that at the margin, airlines are earning a yield on capital higher than our discount rate. This runs somewhat counter to our general argument on the optimal management of companies, and as such could be open to question.

Railway

The calculations on railway capital and operating costs and revenues are based on the high cost investment strategy. This has very much the same characteristics as the tunnel, that is, once built it is relatively inflexible. This explains why the reduction in volume turns a small profit into a fairly substantial loss. As we noted earlier, the analysis of a less sensitive rail strategy does not appear to have been carried out in any great detail. In addition to the effects on the railway itself and on the other organizations listed in the present analysis, a particularly important factor would seem to be noise (*see* page 133).

Ports

Detailed calculations were carried out on both the capital and operating costs of the ports the throughput of which would be influenced by the construction of the tunnel. The most striking aspect of the result is that the loss of fairly substantial turnover produces no overall loss to the ports. This is apparently because major port development would be required at Dover, Folkestone, Harwich and Southampton if the tunnel were not to be built. This investment would offset the economies of scale which might otherwise have been hoped for from the growth of traffic.

Road freight operators

Changes in costs and revenues for road freight operators were calculated but it was assumed that the optimal management assumption held. The consultants expressed this in the following terms: 'It has been assumed that road transport operators' charges will, on average, be similar to their long-term costs including an allowance for asset replacement and also for a commercial return on capital employed'. For this reason the net effect in Table 10.7 is zero.

Road infrastructure

Since the tunnel terminal will be located close to one of the main Channel ports, and since it was assumed that if the tunnel were not built would use these ports instead the total cost of road access was estimated to be broadly the same whether the tunnel was constructed or not. However, there were a number of minor differences and their cost was estimated by the Department of the Environment.

Savings to business passengers

As we saw in the discussion of the Third London Airport, both costs and time savings to business passengers are resource savings to their employers and are naturally expressed in monetary terms. In the case of the channel tunnel, the consultants used similar time values to those adopted by the Roskill Commission, that is, £2.10 an hour in 1980 rising to £2.82 per hour in 1990.

Savings on freight

Savings were calculated separately for roll on/roll off traffic and for containers. In the case of roll on/roll off the figures were as follows.

Benefit due to lower tariffs	£10 per vehicle
Four hour time saving	£6 per vehicle
Total saving	£16 or £1.07 per ton

These benefits were credited to all roll on/roll off traffic which would have travelled through the Dover area in any event. Traffic attracted to this area through the existence of the tunnel was assumed to make a saving of half this amount; this is a similar argument to the one given on page 116. It assumes an equal distribution of traffic over the whole range between those for whom the advantage is the full £1.07 and those who change with a very marginal advantage.

In the case of containers, the tunnel was compared with the service from Harwich to Zeebrugge as no fully equipped container facilities exist or are planned at Dover. In this case the saving was £2.00 per ton.

Cost and time savings to leisure passengers

Three groups of passengers were analysed separately, that is, those accompanying their cars, those without cars and those in coaches.

For passengers accompanying their cars, the saving was the difference in total generalized cost made up as follows.

(a) The cross channel fare including an appropriate proportion of the total fare.

(b) The cost of motoring in the United Kingdom based on a distance cost of 0.53p per passenger mile and a time cost of 23p per hour. The cost per passenger mile was based on a perceived cost of 1.70p per car mile[19]. The time cost was converted to a cost per mile using an average speed of 45 miles an hour.

(c) The cost of motoring on the continent was considered to some extent part of the holiday, and was therefore only costed at half the price of travel in the United Kingdom.

(d) The time spent crossing the channel was valued at the standard rate of 23p per hour. This time included an allowance for waiting time equal to half the service frequency.

This treatment is very similar to that employed in the other studies we have described with the exception of the allowances for waiting time. One would have thought that for journeys of this kind, with a booked service (the present situation) passengers would have scheduled their arrival to relate in some way to the departure which they intended to take. If this were true, the waiting time would be independent of the frequency. It is however not easy to see to what extent an alternative treatment would affect the outcome as the individual components of the user benefits do not appear to have been shown separately in any of the published material.

The generalized cost for independent through rail or air passengers included only the fare and the journey time evaluated at 23p per hour. In the case of coach passengers, the situation was not modelled in detail and a broad assumption was made of a saving of 50 pence per passenger due to a reduction in journey time.

Sensitivity analysis

The consultants carried out a variety of sensitivity analyses on the following alternative assumptions.

(a) A lower growth of overall traffic. This was clearly necessary in view of the basic uncertainty over the growth of such traffic when considering a period as far away as 1980 or 1990. Whilst the alternative forecast used may represent a reasonable minimum, it is perhaps unfortunate that no more serious long-term forecasting exercise was carried out, particularly with regard to accompanied cars.

(b) A variety of changes in policy by ship operators.

(c) An extension of the construction period of the tunnel by 2 years, and an increase in its capital cost by 20 per cent.

(d) An improvement in the operating costs of ships and aircraft as a result of technological or productivity improvements.

(e) Halving the user benefits to eliminate the value of time to leisure passengers.

None of these sensitivity tests taken individually were sufficient to reduce the net present value of the project to zero, and with the reservations that we have made over the forecasting of traffic, the case for construction of the tunnel appears strong in terms of the analysis carried out. To put the issue of accompanied cars in proportion, it should be noted that the central traffic assumption gives growth to total traffic (that is, tunnel and ferries) from four million passengers in 1971 to 19 million passengers in 1990; the sensitivity analysis carried out reduces this 19 million by some 25 per cent, that is, to approximately 15 million.

Comment

We believe that this study represents a careful and workmanlike analysis of the construction of a major transport link. However, in our view three important criticisms can be levelled against it. These concern the forecasting of traffic, the range of the considerations taken into account and the alternatives considered.

Forecasting of traffic

We have already referred to this problem, particularly in the context of accompanied cars. The project is for the construction of one large inflexible element of transport infrastructure. The sensitivity analysis already carried out has shown that this would be particularly sensitive to errors of traffic forecasting. We consider, therefore, that the statistical exercises carried out could, with advantage, have been supplemented by a rather more creative approach covering such aspects as fly/drive and the impact of increased congestion in holiday areas on the propensity to use cars for holidays at all.

Considerations taken into account

Although the published study was something of a hybrid, the work was originally conceived as a financial exercise on behalf of the investors in the channel tunnel. Its scope was later extended to cover the principal economic interests concerned but this left out the environmental impact of the decision. The most obvious aspect of this omission concerns the high investment rail strategy the justification of which appears to be somewhat sketchy. In addition to the savings of time mentioned in the report, it is likely that a new railway line through the relatively highly populated area between London and the South Coast would cause considerable noise nuisance and this should be evaluated. It is of course true that some of the traffic concerned would be diverted from existing air routes, and that the project should be credited with any relief which this might procure.

Alternative solutions

Perhaps the most interesting area of alternative solutions which was not considered concerns freight. As we have seen, freight shippers base their decisions on the costs which are borne by them and do not include the impact of those decisions on the environment. It would perhaps have been worthwhile investigating an alternative strategy for freight based on the use of ports outside the South East. For example, the transfer of container traffic from the Harwich/Zeebrugge route to the tunnel may not be the unqualified blessing which the analysis portrayed it to be.

From the point of view of this book, the most serious of these observations concerns the environment. As we have seen, one of the great advantages of cost benefit when compared with earlier methods of analysis is that it tries to give a comprehensive picture of any decision. The use of the term to describe work which is basically only economic analysis is, in our view, regrettable. Whilst it is a considerable step forward to extend the scope of the study from a single enterprise to cover all economic interests, this is only part of the story. It seems particularly strange that the Department of the Environment should have published what it described as cost benefit work, and defined the terms of reference specifically to exclude environmental considerations.

11

Industrial Location Decisions

This chapter sets out two further examples concerned with industrial location decisions.

FACTORY IN THE UNITED KINGDOM

Description of project

The company concerned has reached the limit of its production facilities in its existing factory, and long-term plans show that a major new investment will be required over the coming five years. The choice of location of these facilities has been narrowed down to three possibilities.

1. Extension of the existing plant; this has the advantage that it keeps distribution costs, working capital, and factory indirect expenses to a minimum. However, the company's management is rather concerned to see 'so many eggs in one basket'.

2. A site in one of the Government's development areas; this would procure a number of advantages in terms of development area grants on both plant and buildings.

3. A third site which would not be in a development area but in which land

could be acquired cheaply and which would be much better located for distribution.

The evaluation was carried out from the point of view of the company (that is, following normal industrial practice) and used the company's 'cut-off rate' for such projects, of 15 per cent after tax.

Summary of results

The results are given in Table 11.1; figures are relative to the existing factory.

	New site (£'000)	
	Development area	*Non-development area*
Capital lost		
Land	—	30
Labour	31	(18)
Other	—	—
Working capital	(28)	(15)
Direct production costs		
Labour	8	(9)
Other	—	—
Indirect production costs	(18)	(18)
Distribution costs	(53)	(21)
Development area grant	22	—
Total costs	(38)	(51)
Tax	5	30
Value of security	60	60
Total net profit	27	39

Table 11.1

If the question of security were ignored the best solution would be to extend the existing factory. Differences in net present value between this and the other two possibilities are shown in Table 11.2.

The value of the security provided by having two factories rather than one was estimated at £60 000; if this is included, the siting of the factory in the non-development area becomes the most attractive by £39 000.

In this table figures in brackets represent losses relative to the extension of the existing factory.

<table>
<tr><td></td><td colspan="3" align="center">*All figures are in £'000s*</td></tr>
<tr><td></td><td>*Costs*</td><td>*Tax credit*</td><td>*£'000s Net*</td></tr>
</table>

	Costs	Tax credit	£'000s Net
Development area	(38)	5	(33)
Other area	(51)	30	(21)

Table 11.2

Comments on the evaluation

From the company's point of view

The following comments can be made about the summary table.

1   In valuing land it is irrelevant whether the company already owned it or not. A common error is to take into account only cash payments and to include the cost of the land for a new site but exclude it for an existing one on which the company has surplus space. The argument for including the 'opportunity cost' in both cases, is that the company could sell existing land if it were not to be used for the new project or alternatively could use it for a project that would otherwise require the acquisition of new land.

2   Differences in labour cost are usually fairly easy to estimate for the present situation; however, as we are interested in forecasts it is important to bear in mind the possible impact on the labour market of a large new factory.

3   In this case the setting up of a new factory caused increases in working capital, due largely to the splitting of raw material stocks between the two sites. This would, however, depend upon the way in which products were allocated between the two sites. This company had decided to set up a 'mirror image' factory on the new site for security reasons.

4   The item, 'indirect expenses', corresponded to a belief that there were economies of scale in factory management; such beliefs are very widespread and by no means always justified. Assumptions on these lines therefore require careful examination.

5   In the evaluation of distribution costs, it is most important that the situation should be 'sub-optimized'. It could well be that the building of a new factory would be the signal to re-examine the whole distribution system, the location of depots, etc, and that an evaluation carried out in

the existing framework would automatically disfavour anything new.

6   The tax figures deserve two comments. First, in the context of a profit-able company it is correct to credit tax on any losses caused by a project; alternatively the profit brought about by a new project can be assumed to pay tax. However, this treatment would not be correct if the entire company were so far into the red that no new projects would involve tax payments. Second, it is interesting to notice the difference in effective tax rate between the two solutions. The much higher credit in the case of the 'non-development' area, is due to the fact that the loss excluding the cost of land is not £51 000 but £81 000. As land purchases are not depreciated for tax there is no charge on the corresponding profit.

7   The item 'security' is not an intangible in the sense in which this word has been used in the presentation of cost benefit analysis. However, it is interesting in that it represents an attempt by the company to take into account the uncertainty of the future. The sum was derived in the following way (Table 11.3).

	£'000s
Annual sales	30 000
Fluctuating margins	35%
Loss of margin on 1 week's sales	200
Probable annual loss after tax at 50%	6
Capitalization of loss after tax	60

Table 11.3

Fluctuating margins were defined as gross sales less raw material and direct labour; it is an appropriate measure when examining very short term 'fluctuations' in sales, but would in many cases be quite inappropriate for more long-term movements.

It was assumed that there was a 3 per cent probability of events leading to the loss of a complete week's sales; these included a local strike and a local health hazard involving the company's food products. Furthermore it was assumed that the loss would grow at 5 per cent a year; discounting at 15 per cent a year and summing to infinity, the resulting estimate was as shown.

From the community's point of view

A number of interesting points can be made on the results of this analysis from the community's point of view.

1   The factory could have an effect on local unemployment. Suppose that

this existed in the non-development area and that the additional expenditure of £27 000 in this respect simply related to people who would not otherwise have been employed. The community would add this item back; thus, if this were the only change, it would make the non-development area best even before taking tax into account.

2   The two new sites have been penalized by the effect of additional stockholdings of raw materials. This is usually identical with the national interest but not always; if the stocks concerned related to domestic agricultural products that would be stored somewhere in the country in any event, this would no longer be true.

3   If the development area grant represents the gain to the community resulting from the installation of the factory, this is a legitimate item in the evaluation. It is a way of making social costs appear in the calculations carried out by companies and should not be eliminated under the rule that it is a transfer payment. Another interesting case is that of rates. This is a form of taxation which corresponds in principle to services rendered by the local authority. However, in practice, these services may be more or less than the rates bill and in such cases the payment by the company should be replaced by the actual resource costs incurred.

An example of this latter point occurred during the discussion of the British Airports Authority's profits at the Roskill Commission; then it claimed that rates payment ought not to be taken into account as they were purely a question of taxation; the counter argument was the one just given: that they corresponded to services. This question of selective taxation designed to put monetary values on various aspects of government policy and, to reflect social values, is discussed in Chapter 14.

4   Tax on profits. From the community's point of view the evaluation should be carried out before tax, and therefore this item would be removed. In the absence of other changes it is interesting to note that this would have reversed the order of preference between the development area and the other area. This is because of the influence of the purchase of land referred to in the previous section.

5   Discount rate. If the future were known, the community would discount the various items in the evaluation at 10 per cent and not at the 15 per cent after tax or 25 per cent before tax used by the company. This would have the effect of increasing the importance of future payments relative to present ones and in particular would improve the development area solution in this problem. However, the use of high rates of discount by commercial firms may correspond to the fact that their executives are habitually over optimistic. Such an argument would not seem to be applicable in the present case, as it is not dealing with such things as sales

estimates but rather with terms that it is in nobody's interest to exaggerate or to minimize.

The use by industry of rates substantially higher than those recommended by the Government for financial evaluations is also discussed in the concluding chapter.

An interesting practical case in which two different interest rates caused a decision to be reversed was the building of a bridge to link the Isle of Re with the mainland of France. A cost benefit analysis was carried out on behalf of the central Government and this showed that the project would be viable using the then ruling rate of 10 per cent. However, the local authority who would have had to build and finance the project stated that their cut-off rate for such schemes was 14 per cent and that the investment was no longer valid on this basis.

The notion of cut-off rate is an interesting one; it is essentially a function of the supply and demand of capital and may be very high if, for one reason or another, a company has not got access to capital at attractive interest rates. If it has a large number of projects and a fixed amount of capital, the cut-off rate is the rate such that there are projects available costing a total equal to this of capital and all having yields equal to or greater than the cut-off rate.

INDUSTRIAL INVESTMENT IN AN UNDERDEVELOPED COUNTRY

Many companies have found unforeseen difficulties when seeking to invest in underdeveloped countries. This is partly because the criteria for such investment are not the same as those in more developed areas, and governments are usually preoccupied with difficult foreign exchange situations. Therefore it is most important that any company envisaging such an investment should attempt to look at it from the point of view of the local government, that is, carry out a limited cost benefit analysis.

This problem was faced on a very large scale by the United Africa Company, a subsidiary of Unilever, in its investments in the 1960s and the following example, although not directly connected with any specific investment, draws on experience gained when working with their company. It was necessary to convince not only the investor, the Board of the United Africa Company, but also the local government, of the attractiveness of any proposition. The interesting thing is that these two interests, which occasionally appeared to be in conflict, were by no means necessarily so. A sound industrial investment, even when it implies substantial dividend repatriation, can be very good value for the receiving country.

Description of the project

The company had been importing a range of toilet preparations for many years;

	Company's viewpoint		Country's viewpoint			
			Imports		Local manufacture	
	Imports	Local manufacture	Foreign exchange	Local exchange	Foreign exchange	Local exchange
Production costs UK	(151)	—	(151)	—	—	—
Freight, insurance, handling	(40)	—	(40)	—	—	—
Customs duty	(25)	—	—	—	—	—
Local production costs						
Labour	—	(40)	—	—	—	—
Local subcontracts	—	(20)	—	—	—	(5)
Local raw material	—	(50)	—	—	—	(20)
Imports c.i.f.	—	(40)	—	—	(40)	—
duty	—	(20)	—	—	—	—
Training costs	—	(15)	—	—	(15)	—
Total cost ex-factory	(216)	(185)	(191)	—	(55)	(25)
Marketing	(24)	(18)	(5)	(10)	(5)	(5)
Distribution	(30)	(23)	(10)	(20)	(7)	(14)
General administration	(20)	(18)	(10)	(5)	(12)	(3)
Total cost	(290)	(244)	(216)	(35)	(79)	(47)
Sales	300	300		300		225
Profit	10	56				
Tax	(5)	(28)				
Investments and working capital	(5)	(18)	(5)	—	(6)	(3)
Dividends/capital	—	10	(6)	—	(10)	—
Benefit to country: gross			(227)	265	(95)	(3)
net				38	80	175

TABLE 11.4

these were manufactured by its associate in England. In the past this trade was extremely profitable but margins had been squeezed by pressure from two sources.

1   Other competitive importers.

2   Resistance to price increases by the local government and suggestions by them that local manufacturing plant should be set up. They indicated that even if this should result in higher prices due to less efficient manufacturing conditions, they would be prepared to accept consumer price increases and would also raise tariffs on imports to such a level that these would be effectively excluded.

The main product line was sold at 15D; it had been assumed that in order to be profitable with local manufacture this would be raised to 20D and that sales would fall by 25 per cent as a result leaving total receipts unchanged.

Results of analysis

The problem was analysed from the point of view of the company and of the local government. In both cases a discount rate of 15 per cent before tax was used. (It is often the case that because of supply and demand of capital in underdeveloped countries, the cut-off rate for public investment is considerably higher than in more developed ones.) The results given in Table 11.4 show that local manufacture would be in the interests of the company and of the local community; the gain in net present value is as follows.

	mD
The company	10
The local community	42

The company's position was recalculated using its more usual rate of 15 per cent after tax. The increase in net present value was exactly zero; that is, the internal rate of return of the project was 15 per cent, and this was thought to be acceptable.

A technical point that should be noted in Table 11.4 is the existence of the line 'investment and working capital'; the general development of the theory has referred only to cash payments and receipts; however, in the normal accounting of a company some of these payments and receipts are carried in the balance sheet for a while before being passed into the profit and loss account. For example, machinery and other assets are capitalized and then written off over their expected life. In an industrial context it is often useful to stick to this accounting presentation, and this involves separating out lines in our calculation relating to investments and working capital. An alternative presentation is to include in the costs an interest charge on such working capital and investments using the overall discount rate. It should be noted that if the actual interest paid on overdrafts to finance working capital is higher than the discount rate this procedure will overestimate the profitability of the project; it underestimates the cost of the finance actually employed.

Discussion of results

We will first discuss the results line by line.

Production costs

It is assumed that in the case of local manufacture, costs will completely disappear in Britain. Providing the transfer of production is properly planned, this is usually the case; however, in some circumstances local manufacture may make some items of usable plant redundant and therefore their costs should be shown to continue. It should be noted that this is not concerned with whether the plant has been written off in the books; what counts is the question: 'Could the plant be used to continue manufacture and will it in fact be reusable for some other product?'

Further we have assumed that the exported products were charged at cost. In the present case this is so and is the result of the pressure on profit margins. In the more general case one would expect to see profits in Britain, and these should be added to the local profits in any overall comparison. For example, if there had been a profit element of 20 in the production costs of 151 in the present case, this would not have altered the evaluation from the local government's point of view, but would have made the importing solution more attractive from the point of view of the company. (Profits from imports would then have been 20 in Britain as against 10 in the underdeveloped country under local manufacture.) British production costs and profit appear as foreign exchange costs to the local government.

Freight, insurance and handling

The full cost of freight, insurance and handling has been shown as being a foreign exchange charge for the local government; this would not be true if the goods were to be shipped on a local boat; they would then appear as local costs. Furthermore, if this shipping line were not operating to full capacity, we would not be able to make the assumption of optimal management, and the cost might well be offset by an increase in the profits of this line. In an extreme case the marginal cost of shipping to the developing country might be zero.

Customs duty

Customs duty is a cost to the importer but not to the local government; it could be that under some circumstances a small part of the duty is needed to cover the marginal cost of administering the Customs system; in this case a small charge would remain as local expenditure from the country's point of view.

Local labour costs

The local labour costs, which appear in the company's books, have been eliminated in the national evaluation as it is assumed that there is considerable unemployment.

Local subcontractors

One of the advantages of a scheme of this kind is that it has a multiplier effect on local industry. For this reason the cost of local subcontractors has been reduced from the twenty that appear in the company's books to five. Under certain circumstances the Government might even wish to attach an additional benefit to the generation of local employment and actually treat this not as a charge but as a positive benefit in its own 'book'.

Local raw material

Here it is assumed that the majority of the cost of the local raw material is represented by labour; this is eliminated in the national evaluation on the unemployment argument.

Training costs

It is assumed that these costs will be paid by the local company; they represent local technicians and managers who will be sent to Europe on training courses. Such courses are often one of the big attractions of local industry from the Government's point of view, and once again they might wish to apply some factor to this cost to represent the additional gain to the community from the setting up of a body of skilled industrial workers.

Indirect expenses

The costs of marketing, distribution and general administration fall with local manufacture because of the lower volume of goods caused by an increase in the selling price. From the local community's point of view, part of these costs are in foreign exchange (for example, repatriation of foreign managers' salaries, imports of petrol, vehicles, and so on, for distribution) and part are local; this local element is not counted in fully by the Government as part of it represents labour costs which are not 'real'.

Sales

Under local manufacture prices increase by one third and volume decreases by 25 per cent; therefore total sales taken up by the company are constant. However, the local community applies sound cost benefit techniques and only evaluates the company's receipts at the old selling price. It should be noted that the difference between the 300mD used by the company and the 225mD recognized by the Government is equal to the additional cost imposed by the price increases on consumers who continue to buy toilet preparations. As we noted in our theoretical development this additional cost does not add to their satisfaction.

Profit

The discounted net profit margin before tax of the company goes up by 46mD as a result of the change; however, from this we must deduct the present value of tax payments and also the investments in fixed assets and working capital. The result is given in the line dividends/capital, which is the present value of all the financial transactions between the local subsidiary and its parent. From the country's point of view the notion of profit has to be modified; as we have seen tax is not included in the evaluation as this is a transfer payment. However, the payment of dividends by the company appears as a loss to the country.

Benefits to the country

In spite of the payment of dividends the country is very much better off with local manufacture than without it. Whereas foreign exchange expenditure has gone down by 132mD, local satisfaction has only dropped by 90mD. Under circumstances of excessive foreign exchange stringency the Government might even wish to increase the relative value of the foreign exchange saving and thus show an even greater benefit to the nation. If the market in foreign exchange were free this would appear as a devaluation.

Summary

It is most important in such cases that the investor should be able to produce analyses of this kind to persuade local governments that a given investment is in the interests of an underdeveloped country, even though it involves exporting foreign exchange in the form of dividends. It is interesting to note that although the locally produced toilet preparations were very much more expensive than the imported ones, even including the cost of freight and Customs duty, much of this is not a real cost in the sense that it represents labour that would otherwise be unemployed or underemployed.

12

Two Applications of
Multi-Criteria Analysis

INTRODUCTION

This chapter describes two applications of multi-criteria methods which have recently been carried out in France. These are based on the ideas set out in Chapter 3. The first concerns the choice of alignment for a motorway in the suburbs of a large city, and the second the procedure for judging a town planning competition at Evry near Paris. In such cases, the aim was to find a procedure lying between the following two unacceptable extremes.

1   A classic cost benefit exercise involving the valuation of each criterion in terms of money. In the town planning example such a calculation was impossible in view of the very large number of variables between the solutions considered. In the case of the motorway alignment, one of the major differences between projects was the effect on areas of park-like forest; these were at the centre of the problem, and no satisfactory method could be found of expressing them in monetary terms.

2   A completely unquantified discussion of the issues. This was particularly daunting for the choice of town planning solutions as there were a number of juries and technical commissions involved, requiring a reasoned framework for discussion if any progress was to be made.

In both cases the procedure used made the maximum use of the information

Motorway Alignment Solutions

		1	2	3	4	5	6	7
(1)	Distance	0	0	−0.6	+3.9	+3.4	+4.9	+4.9
(2)	Town Planning	4	4	4	6	6	0	0
(3)	Cost	511	594	1100	927	682	1104	664
(4)	Inhabitants with severe noise	7.5	5.7	4.1	3.2	4.4	4.0	5.3
(5)	Inhabitants with some noise	53	40	25	36	36	23	23
(6)	Historic sites	2	2	2	2	3	2	4
(7)	Hectars of forest destroyed	400	400	370	60	70	20	20
(8)	Hectars of forest affected	880	880	670	30	30	0	0
(9)	Forests affected	2	2	0	0	0	0	0

TABLE 12.1

available, and then compared projects two at a time leading to statements such as the following.

A is definitely better than B and this relationship is accepted by all concerned.

A is probably better than B.

A could be better than B.

A and B cannot be compared.

These statements can be thought of in terms of a range of values for each of the criteria, for example, the statements made in the motorway study when comparing the number of hectars of forest affected and the effect of a longer route on travellers.

'Scarcely anybody would accept the sacrifice of more than 100 hectars of forest to reduce the length of the motorway by five kilometres even for 50 million users per year.'

'Scarcely anybody would refuse to sacrifice five hectars of forest to save five kilometres.'

The statement that A is definitely better than B means that such a comparison would be true taking into account the extreme values of all such ranges for the different criteria. The second statement would mean that the comparison was true for the vast majority of the ranges and so on.

CHOICE OF MOTORWAY ALIGNMENT

This problem is still highly confidential and for this reason it is not possible to disclose the name of the town and the solutions are simply coded.

The first three solutions involved a large amount of damage to forests and other areas of natural beauty; the three alternatives varied as to their precise alignment, and also to the possibility of putting some parts of the motorway underground. The next two alternatives (four and five) involved a somewhat longer journey, a very much worse effect on the general town planning situation, and, in addition, in cost and numbers of inhabitants exposed to noise. The last two solutions represented an even longer route.

Each solution was classified according to the following criteria and the classification of these various criteria is given in Table 12.1.

1   Length of journey.

2   Effect on town planning; for this purpose the different schemes were ranked on a seven point scale (zero very good and six very bad).

3   Cost.

4   Number of inhabitants exposed to heavy noise.

5   Number of inhabitants moderately exposed to noise.

6   Number of major historic buildings affected.

7   Number of hectars of forest destroyed.

8   Number of hectars of forest affected.

9   Number of major woods destroyed.

Working closely with the client a number of ranges of values were decided upon including the one relating hectars of forest to journey length described in the introduction.   Using these the team was able to set up the following diagram (*Figure 12.1*) of relationships between solutions.

From *Figure 12.1* we can make the following statements: all the 'forest' solutions (1, 2 and 3) are worse than solution (4).   Furthermore solutions (1) and (2) are almost certainly worse than (5), and solution (3) is worse than (6). We are not able to make statements with any certainty about comparisons between solutions (4), (5), (6) and (7) (the non-forest solutions).   The only indication is that (4) is better than (6).

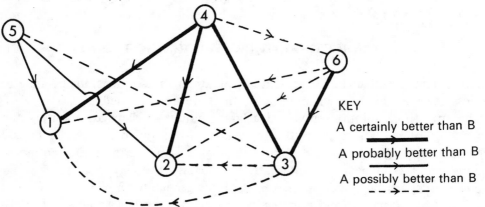

KEY

A certainly better than B

A probably better than B

A possibly better than B

Figure 12.1   *Diagram of relationships – motorway alignments*

Our overall conclusion is therefore that the study can concentrate on the solutions not involving forest.   The range of values relating forests to the other considerations is very large (roughly 1 to 20); nevertheless, this is sufficient to enable us to make positive statements relating to all three forest solutions.

TOWN PLANNING COMPETITION

Six firms of architects had submitted schemes for the competition for a major scheme at Evry, south of Paris. Although the basic methods used were similar to those in the previous case, their application was slightly more sophisticated using the computer model ELECTRE. For each comparison between two possibilities, this calculates the following.

1　A concord coefficient. This is the degree of agreement that project A is better than project B. It not only depends upon being able to classify each project on each criterion, but also upon the attribution of a weighting for each criterion. This can be shown in the following example (Table 12.2).

	Criteria		
	A	B	C
Weighting	50%	35%	15%
Project A	11	18	5
Project B	10	2	14

Table 12.2

Project A is better than project B on the two criteria A and B. The concord indicator is calculated as being 50 plus 35 equals 85 per cent, that is, the sum of the weightings of the criteria for which A is better than B. It should be noted that this notion of concord is based on the relative values of the scores and not on the scores themselves. The result would have been the same if project A had been scored 12, 15 and seven.

　The programme defined a threshold for concord (for example 70 per cent) as a basis for the statement A is better than B.

2　Discord. The aim of this discord factor is to ensure that A's inferiority on the criteria for which it is not better than B, is not sufficiently large as to invalidate the comparison indicated by concord. In this case the discord function was fairly complex.

In the first case considered, the method was applied in two stages. Firstly by the jury looking at the project as a whole, and secondly by a number of technical commissions. From the point of view of the method, these two steps were very similar; therefore, we will only describe the procedure adopted by the jury.

　The scores obtained for each project and the calculations of concord and discord are given in Tables 12.3 and 12.4. A number of tables of the relationships between the projects were then drawn up using different threshold values for concord and discord. In almost all of these a stable pattern of relationships

Scores

		1	2	3	4	5	6	7	Average
(1)	General capacity	11.8	13.3	14.7	9.7	15.7	10.5	14.8	12.9
(2)	Reliability of programme	9.2	12.3	11.4	11.7	12.4	12.1	11.5	11.5
(3)	Qualities of town	7.8	12.7	10.3	11.3	15.7	10.8	12.4	11.4
	housing	7.3	13.1	10.1	12.3	15.7	10.8	12.6	11.7
	public investment	7.0	13.6	8.6	8.8	15.1	9.7	12.8	10.6
	commerce	8.7	13.5	13.3	11.8	13.5	9.8	12.1	11.8
	employment	9.6	13.5	12.0	12.6	13.4	11.0	12.5	12.1
	traffic	8.6	10.5	10.6	12.3	14.2	11.2	11.9	11.3
	functional links	7.7	13.3	10.8	11.6	14.9	12.1	11.8	11.2
	planning	8.0	11.3	10.6	9.5	15.2	11.0	12.9	11.2
	development	7.7	10.1	9.2	12.4	11.7	10.4	12.2	10.6
	Weighted average	9.1	12.5	11.7	10.9	14.5	11.0	12.8	11.7
	Ranking	7	3	4	6	1	5	2	–

Table 12.3

Concord and Discord (The Figures in Parenthesis Denote Discord)

Dominating Projects	Dominated Projects						
	1	2	3	4	5	6	7
1		12.2 (2.8)	10.2 (2.1)	15.5 (0.7)	0.1	15.8 (1.5)	4.5 (2.9)
2	86.1 (0.4)		58.7 (0.7)	56.6 (0.4)	20.9 (2.15)	65.0 (0.61)	47.1 (1.2)
3	85.2 (0.5)	33.8 (1.5)		38.6 (0.4)	16.7 (2.2)	44.5 (0.4)	32.7 (1.4)
4	81.1 (1.4)	39.0 (2.3)	54.0 (2.7)		9.7 (7.6)	44.0 (0.6)	23.5 (1.4)
5	99.8 (0.0)	72.5 (0.5)	79.4 (0.5)	85.0 (0.1)		89.7 (0.0)	73.3 (0.6)
6	82.1 (0.7)	30.7 (1.6)	49.5 (2.4)	43.8 (1.6)	5.7 (2.5)		22.5 (1.4)
7	92.1 (0.4)	46.9 (0.8)	61.7 (0.7)	69.4 (0.7)	21 (1.6)	74.2 (0.7)	

Table 12.4

emerged which is summarized in *Figure 12.2*. This showed that there was a positive relationship between project (6) and all the other projects, project (6) being better. However, projects (2) and (8) could not be compared although they were both worse than project (6), and both better than all the other projects. Similarly, there was no comparison between projects (3), (5) and (7).

The conclusions to be drawn from *Figure 12.2* were that in the absence of better information, project (6) was the best. However, if we were looking for a short list of three projects, we could choose (2), (6) and (8). In the event of looking for a short list of four projects, it would not be possible to go forward at this stage as such a short list could either be projects (2), (6), (8) and (3); (2), (6), (8) and (5) or (2), (6), (8) and (7).

The organization of such a competition is a complex matter; in this case there were 17 members of the jury and five technical commissions made up of between ten and 30 people, plus the competitors themselves and the officers of the organization responsible for carrying out the work. Although not all these people were convinced by the method, most found it useful to introduce some such framework into their reasoning. In particular it enabled internal conflicts and discrepancies to be resolved in a logical manner while maintaining the essential uncertainty on certain aspects of the data.

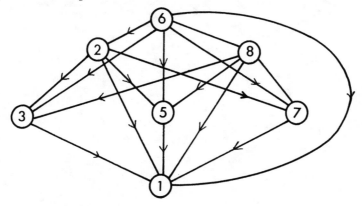

Figure 12.2 *Diagram of relationships – town planning competition*

CONCLUSION

Both the problems treated in this chapter were complex issues involving a number of totally different criteria. Discussion of them had tended to polarize into a situation of open conflict between partisans of the different points of view. In the case of the motorway, this was largely between conservationists who wished to preserve forests and the more traditional highway analysts. In the case of the town planning competition, there was conflict between those concerned with houses, public investment, commerce, employment, traffic, capacity for development and so on.

In each case the approach was based on defining areas of concensus. Although basic conflicts remained, these were irrelevant to some comparisons. Although conservationists valued forests twenty times more than traffic engineers, this did not affect the final result. The degree of progress that could be made on the basis of such notions was limited, however, and some comparisons were not possible. Nevertheless, this should not be seen as a criticism of the method, but rather as a way of showing the fundamental insufficiency of the data. In particular it highlighted areas in which further study was required, and avoided wasting resources on those which were irrelevant to the problem.

The two cases examined raised different facets of this problem. In the first, the issue was essentially one of values; the authorities concerned made up a small group of individuals but they were faced with a problem which seemed to be completely intractable. In the second case on the other hand, the main problem was to bring some order into the work of a large number of people faced with a difficult problem in an area where, traditionally, judgement had been extremely subjective. In both cases it seems reasonable to claim a degree of success based on the application of multi-criteria methods. The reason for this success is that such methods, although quite elaborate in their development, are firmly based on common sense.

13

Other Applications of Cost Benefit Analysis

The Roskill Commission was unusual in two respects: a very complete analysis was produced before any decision was taken, and, with the exception of certain items concerning defence, the whole of this work was published. It is extremely difficult to find other equally satisfactory examples; however, an interesting one in Britain is provided by Foster and Beesley's work on the Victoria Line in London.

The example of town planning at St Etienne and the one concerning railway inspection in this chapter were used as part of the decision-making process; however, they were not the object of public discussion on the lines of the Roskill Commission and therefore less detail is available on them.

The other two examples in Chapter 11 concern private companies and therefore have not been published.

BUILDING AN UNDERGROUND RAILWAY

In August 1962 the British Treasury authorized the building of a new underground railway from Walthamstow in North-East London. This was the first new underground to be built in London since 1914. It was apparent, however, that the revenue for the London Transport authority would not be sufficient to cover the cost of this undertaking without substantial price increases, and a very imaginative exercise was carried out by Foster and Beesley[14] to show how the Victoria Line might be justified on social grounds.

Victoria Line

£m discounted at 6% p.a.

Economic terms

    Profits

Underground railway		
Working expenses of Victoria Line (VL)	(16.2)	
Capital expenditure (less terminal saving value)	(38.5)	
Cost savings	1.7	
Increased revenue	18.1	(34.9)
British Railways		6.1
London Transport buses		7.3
General business		—
Total		(21.5)

Expenditure which brings no satisfaction	
Gross savings to motorists who transfer to VL	8.0
Gross savings to motorists who do not transfer	8.9
Fare savings on generated traffic	1.3
Fares paid to LT	(18.1)
Other	2.3
Total	2.4

Intangibles

Time savings	
Diverted traffic to underground	17.4
Road users, not diverted	21.5
Generated traffic	2.2
Comfort	9.2
Total	50.3
Total	31.2

Table 13.1

The results of this initial analysis, published in 1963, are given in Table 13.1. The layout shown in the table corresponds to the approach used throughout this book; although the figures are substantially those produced by Foster and Beesley they are rearranged with the various terms under the familiar headings of: profit; expenditure that does not affect consumption; and intangibles.

It is interesting to note that the discussion which followed publication of this work was largely centred on the very substantial loss that would be caused for London Transport, and on the ways in which this loss might be met. A possible advantage of our presentation which uses the notion of profit as a key element, is that attention would have been drawn to this financial problem automatically. It is discussed at the end of this section. The analysis calls for the following comments.

1 The need for this investment was quite rightly identified as being largely caused by anomalies in the system of transport pricing. Often road users do not pay the full price for the resources that they consume and, in particular, the congestion and environmental damage that results from their activities.

2 As already mentioned, the profit of the underground railway was not calculated initially; Foster and Beesley's first presentation simply quoted the change in working expenses and capital expenditure resulting from the introduction of the new line. The overall loss of £34.9m emerged from their second paper, when the question of pricing was considered; this included a wide variety of possible methods of financing the line. They arrived at the interesting conclusion that if prices were raised sufficiently to cover the capital cost, the loss of traffic would be such that the investment would no longer be viable from the nation's point of view – although profitable to London Transport. This was essentially linked with the question of road prices; however, it is interesting to note that although the calculation of profit is carried out in constant prices, this does not mean that these prices will not change as a result of the choice. The use of prices that are the same between the two alternatives can be traced back to our original theory about the behaviour of individuals. In particular if they maximize their satisfaction, price is a good measure of marginal utility. However, if prices do actually change, as a result of some economic decision, this will be very relevant as the change may affect demand.

    Similarly, the profits of British Rail were not calculated in the initial report but were introduced later. It was properly suggested that under ideal conditions the railway should pay back to London Transport the windfall gain in profit that had arisen by the building of the new railway. In practice, however, this would be extremely difficult.

3 Business time was not a very large factor in the calculation, as the percentage of passengers affected by the construction of the new line who were travelling on business was in almost all cases less than 5 per cent. The effect on differences in general business profit, because of losses and gains of time, was therefore not evaluated separately.

    It should perhaps be noted that Foster and Beesley used an extremely low valuation of £0.36 an hour for business time; in the light of the Roskill Commission's investigations this should be multiplied by a factor of about eight.

4 Expenditure which brings no satisfaction. The various items adding up to

a total of £2.4m are based on fairly elaborate traffic forecasts. This total represents the overall savings in cost to travellers as a result of the building of the line. In Foster and Beesley's presentation the item 'fares paid to London Transport' did not appear, and the same figure as that shown in the profit calculation has been taken by us. This is almost certainly an oversimplification, as part of these additional fares come from generated traffic; therefore they are not costs borne by people who travel under both alternatives – building and not building. For such generated traffic the general assumption is that the satisfaction produced equals the price paid, and that therefore there is no need to introduce a term. However, in the same way asiin the discussion of the Third London Airport, Foster and Beesley did include a small term (£1.3m) to take into account the fact that the change affecting passengers was not marginal; this corresponds to a calculation of the type:

$$\tfrac{1}{2}\,(t_1 - t_2)\,(c_2 - c_1)$$

where t is the level of traffic and c is the cost to the traveller (*see* Chapter 2).

5   Socio-economic terms. The social credit that would outweigh the cost of this scheme was almost all in the form of travellers' time. Foster and Beesley used £0.25 an hour for leisure time, and £0.36 an hour for business time. These two values were weighted together to take into account the proportion of business travellers – for example, 5 per cent for underground users – and the result applied to time savings arising out of the traffic calculations. These savings came from two main sources.

(a)   The better system of public transport made available to travellers. For many people the construction of the Victoria Line avoided much longer underground rail journeys, combinations of bus and underground, and so on.

(b)   A general increase in traffic speeds because of less congestion in London. An interesting feature of this latter item was that the time differences evaluated were often exceedingly small (5 minutes per passenger journey for motorists); however, because there were so many of these, the overall saving was still very large.

6   Comfort. An interesting term introduced in this study was the notion of comfort, as measured by the possibility of obtaining a seat. The figures finally used, however, were based on a mixture of experience and intuition rather than on any survey data; this, and similar areas, are clearly ones in which further work could be very rewarding.

7   Accident savings and environmental effects of traffic. These two factors

were recognized but not quantified. Once again further research work is needed. A particularly interesting and important aspect in traffic problems is the total noise and pollution nuisance produced by motor vehicles of different types; this could not only be used in evaluations such as those for urban motorways but also in devising and justifying schemes for encouraging manufacturers and users to diminish the noise and fumes output of vehicles.

8   Land values. An interesting point raised by Foster and Beesley is the effect of economic decisions on land values. As they rightly point out, movements in the price of land resulting from an economic change such as a building of a new transport system reflect greater ease of access, and so on. Thus if we have already counted the time savings and other beneficial results to the people using the land, it would be double counting to add the effect on prices as well. It is, however, sometimes appropriate to use the value as a substitute for actual calculations of nuisance; this was the approach used by the Research Team when dealing with noise at the Third London Airport. They reasoned that the reduction in house prices could be used as a measure of the real nuisance suffered. Although, as mentioned in the discussion of the Roskill Commission, this requires careful interpretation, such an approach would be generally correct; however, here it would then be wrong to add a separate estimate of the nuisance (or in this case benefit).

9   Discounting. One of the pieces of sensitivity analysis carried out by Foster and Beesley was to recalculate their results using three different discount rates. In discussing these they pointed out that there were three methods of allowing for risk in such evaluations.

(a)   Recalculating the values of the various terms.
(b)   Varying the life of the project.
(c)   Changing the discount rate.

They chose the first two methods and rejected the discount rate as a treatment of risk. This was probably right, but it is worth noting that it is at odds with the treatment commonly used in industry; here profits (and cash flows in general) are commonly discounted at very high rates such as 25 per cent before tax to allow for risk.

An interesting point made by the paper in this context was the importance of speed in capital works; they showed that it was worth spending up to an additional £4m on capital expenditure if this would enable the period of construction to be reduced by one and a half years. The engineers who are responsible for the preparation of capital projects are often extremely loath to spend money in this way, and many industrial investments have been delayed in a shockingly costly manner, in order to obtain satisfaction on some relatively unimportant point.

TOWN PLANNING IN ST ETIENNE

This example is based on a study carried out in St Etienne, an industrial town, in the centre of France by Sema*. It is also quoted with a much fuller mathematical treatment in J Lesourne's book *Le Calcul Economique*[15].

The background to the analysis was that a general development plan for the town of St Etienne had already been prepared, and a number of suggestions were made as to ways in which it might be improved. These were as follows.

1 S1 a reduction in the density of the centre of the town (all these are relative changes and take as their base the overall plan existing year by year) and moving over 8000 people out to a suburb called Trois Ponts.

2 S2 was a similar project involving another new suburb.

3 CC was a change in the opposite direction; greater densities in the town centre and a slower rate of growth at the Trois Ponts site.

The starting point of the study was to prepare population estimates and in particular to check the consistency of plans with such things as the availability of services, induced tertiary employment, and so on. In these estimates it was assumed that the total population would be unchanged and that the only areas that would be affected were the two new suburbs and the city centre. These estimates are summed up in Table 13.2.

Interesting questions occur in cases such as this, when the total population is not constant. An example arose in the Roskill Commission, where a notional standard value of producing a house and associated services was adopted for regions other than the one under study. Such standards are often required in schemes of this kind, as it may not be possible to say what happens to the population that is gained or lost.

The problem at St Etienne was limited to measuring the cost of providing housing and infrastructure at the various sites, and then measuring the differences in journey times and costs for people living in them. These are summed up in Table 13.3 which calls for the following comments.

Sub-optimization

In comparing plans of this kind it is most important that the planning department should be flexible in its attitude, and be ready to produce outline plans which are

* Société d'Economie et de Mathématiques Appliquées: A large French company in the Metra Group

Population Movements

Solution	New suburbs		City centre
Population	S1	S2	
1975 S1	+8560	−1560	−7000
S2	+1500	+5500	−7000
CC	−5000	−	+5000
1985 S1	+8600	−1600	−7000
S2	+5300	+1700	−7000
CC	−5000	−	+5000

TABLE 13.2

Cost Benefit Comparison

	S1	S2	CC
Profits			
Public transport	− 1	+ 5	− 2
Roads	+27	− 8	+26
Car parks	−63	−78	+ 5
Water board, drains, gas and electricity	−11	−	− 1
Housing	+82	+56	+34
Total	+34	−25	+62
Expenditure with no satisfaction			
Transport	−67	−59	+60
Intangibles			
Time	−57	−42	+20
Total	−90	−126	+142

TABLE 13.3

different from what they had originally envisaged. For example, suppose in this case that a new drainage system had been planned which fitted in with the overall development programme. It could be that maintaining this plan would make one of the proposed solutions (for example, a new suburb) excessively costly, and that a first reaction might be to reject the idea for this reason. However, the inclusion of such a suburb might make it right to redesign future drainage schemes completely. The resulting overall cost might then be substantially lower than the original drainage scheme with the new suburb 'tacked on'. While it is not feasible or economic to study every aspect of a planning operation from first principles, it is nevertheless essential that all large terms in a cost benefit analysis should be subjected to the question: 'Does this additional cost correspond to some intrinsic drawback in the new scheme, or is it simply that it does not "mesh in" with infrastructural arrangements as they are now foreseen?'.

Making realistic outline plans to deal with cases such as this is a very different matter from the detailed planning of a scheme that may be finally decided upon; it requires considerable experience and training, and the willingness to develop overall checks to ensure that the outline scheme is not wildly wrong. Similar situations are met with in industry; for example, if a new capital programme, designed to cope with a certain tonnage, shows an investment per ton that is very different from existing cost levels (perhaps on a replacement cost basis), this should often be viewed with considerable suspicion.

Level of service

A problem that is often met with in planning decisions is the level of service to which the various alternatives should be designed. Obviously it may not be economical to design for the same level in each area; the attainment of, say, a given standard of public transport may be economic in a city centre, but not in the case of a far-flung suburb. In the St Etienne study it was assumed for simplicity that most infrastructural services would be provided to the same level; however, where this is not so, it becomes essential to attach values to the different levels of services provided.

A further example might be the case of mains sewage versus cesspits. Although users may prefer the former, their preference expressed in money terms may not justify the cost of the very considerable public works involved in country districts; to draw up a scheme provising main sewers might automatically exclude solutions that would be perfectly viable on general cost benefit grounds.

Parking and road building

These were two very large items in the St Etienne study, and the remarks on levels of service apply particularly to them. The higher cost of providing parking facilities in the suburbs depends upon the assumption that such parks would be needed in the centre of the town for commuters but not otherwise, and that it would not be public policy to allow people to leave their cars in the street. In the case of roads the problem is still more evident; it would be clearly impossible to provide a road system that would enable those in the suburbs to reach the city centre as quickly as people living there. The corresponding disbenefit item will of course appear in the evaluation of time and travel costs. What is important is that the road system for the suburban sites should give the best possible combination of cost and benefits for that particular solution.

In the case of car parking, the treatment adopted in our presentation is equivalent to assuming that the consumer does not pay for his parking in either case; the difference in cost thus comes out as a loss in the books of the 'parking company'; an alternative treatment would be to show this cost as 'expenditure which causes no satisfaction'. In this particular case a person would be no happier about his car because it was parked in a multistorey building or on a very expensive piece of ground, rather than in a cheap but effective garage beside his house in the country.

Other 'profit terms' were calculated for the provision of water, drainage, gas and electricity; the differences as between the three new possibilities or in comparison with the original scheme are not large.

Unwanted expenditure

The item unwanted expenditure is concerned with travelling costs for people who make a given journey under the two planning solutions that are being compared. Not surprisingly the decentralized solutions come off rather badly in this analysis and the dense city centre rather well. An interesting point is that cost savings in such analyses are generally evaluated excluding the capital cost of cars; an additional factor arises where a combination of clever planning and good public transport leads to large numbers of city dwellers not purchasing cars at all. Here there would obviously be very much greater economies under this item.

Intangibles

In the St Etienne evaluation the only intangible measured was time; this itself was a great advance on earlier planning studies which had been principally concerned with more or less qualitative assessments of the reaction of individuals. However, it is clearly desirable that this treatment should be extended to other intangibles and in particular the effect of commuting traffic on the amenity of towns through levels of pollution, visual effects, and so on. Furthermore one must take into account the qualitative improvement in some aspects of general living conditions that is obtained by moving to suburbs – quiet, view, space, and so on – and of other qualitative improvements that can result from well organized city life; these may largely be in the form of convenience (often another name for time) but may lead to structural changes in people's behaviour over such things as visiting friends, entertainment, and so on.

Conclusions

The quantification of planning decisions is an extremely exciting area. However, in order to be realistic it demand two notable qualities of analysis.

1   A willingness to take into account people's real feelings about living in various conditions. It is no good writing off apparently irrational preferences, such as those shown by East End Londoners moved by the Greater London Council (so interestingly described in *Family and Kinship in the East End of London*[20]); feelings that may seem absurd to the planner should be given as much attention as more 'respectable' economic terms.

2   To take these various factors into account, much more attention has got to be given to problems of measurement. In many studies this has received singularly little attention and has been subordinated to rather intellectual discussion of abstractions. Any marketing executive knows that while attitudes can be influenced, to ignore them leads to catastrophe.

LAW AND REGULATIONS

This example will discuss a second problem that was also suggested by Jacques Lesourne, and for which a mathematical treatment is included in his book *Le Calcul Economique.* This concerns the enforcement of regulations and, in particular, the paying of fares on public transport.

A railway company is particularly concerned by the high percentage of passengers who manage not to pay their fare; at present about one in three of these is caught. This is felt to be the result of the withdrawal of regular inspection of tickets in all trains (as distinct from on the platform) and is particularly acute on one particular line. The company therefore proposes to go back to systematic inspection so as to reduce the chances to one in two. Traffic estimates are given in Table 13.4.

Law Example

(Figures denote 00'000 passengers)

	Existing system	*More inspectors*	*Difference*
Rail passengers			
Fare paying	9.2	10.2	1.0
Non paying			
caught	1.1	0.6	(0.5)
not caught	2.2	0.6	(1.6)
Road travellers	18.7	19.2	0.5
Total	31.2	30.6	(0.6)

Table 13.4

The figures are expressed in terms of discounted passengers. This notion may seem strange but it was found particularly useful in the discussion of the Roskill Commission. It gives a much clearer idea of relative traffic volumes than do year-by-year figures, or totals on an undiscounted basis. In particular, if we are dealing with a term which involves an extra cost of £1 per passenger, the total discounted effect can be readily arrived at by multiplying the discounted traffic by £1.

The effect of the introduction of the new system, based on trials, and experience before the new inspection techniques were introduced, will be to reduce the total number of evasions and to increase the proportion that are caught. Part of the reduction is accounted for by people who will pay for their ticket, part by those who will go over to using their private car and part by individuals so discouraged that they no longer make the trip.

These various movements were evaluated as before to give Table 13.5. Table 13.5 shows that from the railway's point of view the new scheme would be a good idea, but that if we take into account other social effects it is not. This rather 'immoral' result raised the question whether the State had any particular interest in discouraging law breaking beyond its immediate direct economic effects.

A more extreme case arises, for example, where someone steals some money without causing any damage. Under our 'optimal distribution of income' assumption, the State might seem to be indifferent to this transaction. The fact that it is clearly not, means that law breaking is seen as a cost; the very considerable efforts deployed in crime prevention gives us a key as to how this might be measured.

		£00'000
Profits		
The railway		
Additional fares	3.0	
Cost savings	1.2	
Cost of administration of new scheme	(1.3)	
Loss of fines	(2.5)	0.4
Other		–
Consumption that brings no satisfaction		
Costs for those who move to road	0.2	
Additional cost of fines to those who still don't pay	(1.0)	
Additional cost of fares to those who now pay less		
saving on fines	(1.3)	(2.1)
Intangibles		
Time loss to those who go to road	(0.7)	
Psychological savings to those who no longer travel without		
paying	1.5	
Psychological loss to those who still don't pay	(0.1)	0.7
Net cost benefit		(1.0)

Table 13.5

Turning to Table 13.5 itself we find the following terms.

Railway profit

The introduction of the new scheme means that receipts go up on a diminished volume, this increasing profits; however, these are largely absorbed by the cost of administration and the loss of fines. It is worth noticing that if the fines had been payable to a third party (for example, a court) the railway would be much keener to discourage fare evasion, as it would have no interest in the 'proceeds of crime'. It should be noted that the cost saving on the 1.1m loss of passengers is considerably less than the additional revenue from 1.0m additional fare payers. This is because at the margin costs of railways are said to be very much less than the fare. An example was given at the hearings of the Roskill Commission, where marginal costs were held to be about £0.20 per hundred passenger miles compared with fares of approximately £2.

Consumption that brings no satisfaction

This includes three items.

(a)   Those passengers who switch to road transport make a slight saving; this depends very much upon the occupancy of motor cars.

(b)   Those who continue to travel by rail but still do not pay the fine in spite of the new controls can expect to pay more in the form of fines as a result of the increased probability of being caught; one-half of £5 minus one-third of £5.

(c)   Those who now pay fares (£3) and who did not pay under the old system are also faced with higher expenditure.

Time savings

Those passengers who switch to road transport are faced with a longer journey than if they had travelled by rail. This has been evaluated at the leisure rate, in this case £0.25 an hour; it was assumed that all business passengers would in fact pay their fares and that these would not be involved in the switch.

Psychological attitude

The remaining intangible terms in Table 13.5 concerned the psychological attitude of passengers towards not paying their fares. Here it is assumed that, in addition to the expectation of paying a fine, passengers incur a further psychological disbenefit representing the unpleasantness of being caught. Of course, this figure could be negative if people positively enjoy the avoidance of fares, taxes, and so on, and if they would suffer no particular remorse on being caught. There appears to be little valid research data on this subject, but it is clearly of considerable importance when trying to forecast people's reactions to various forms of regulation. Any form of legal enforcement will be much more effective if psychological values are high. In addition to a sense of civic responsibility, factors that are likely to have a considerable influence are the attitudes of other people, the amount of publicity involved, the 'discomfort' incurred through court proceedings, and so on.

Community attitudes

As mentioned in the introduction to this example, a factor that was not taken into account is the attitude of the community to law breaking. While this factor is difficult to quantify there can be no doubt that it exists; work might be based on an examination of existing law-enforcement procedures, that is, the amount of resources that the State is willing to devote in order to ensure that, for example, thefts do not take place.

An interesting example can be found in the system of parking fines in Paris; here the fine is about £2 and the chances of being caught on any one day about one in three. The resulting expected 'parking price' is very close to the cost of leaving a car in a garage, and as a result garages are typically empty and the streets full of parked vehicles. Whether or not this is desirable, the question arises whether people who are in the habit of paying fines of this kind become less law-abiding as a result.

Has the State lost anything ·by breeding a new category of delinquents? Similar questions arise when dealing with most other forms of traffic offences particularly when the administration of the system of fines passes through the same courts as criminal offences.

OTHER APPLICATIONS

We believe that the technique which has been described so far, and which is illustrated by the examples of the last five chapters, is applicable to almost any form of public or corporate decision. In some cases the quantification of benefits may be fairly rough and ready; in others it justifies extensive research. Other problems to which it has been applied are as follows.

Level of service provided by public undertakings

The main characteristic here is that there is no competition and therefore no way of ensuring that the wishes of the consumer are recognized by the authority providing the service. Examples include staffing and queueing problems associated with public offices of various kinds, hospitals, and so on.

Investments designed to reduce dangers to the public

There are a number of well-documented examples concerning the construction of dams to mitigate flood damage, the treatment of rocks overhanging a road, and so on. In some cases almost all the costs and benefits are in the form of 'intangibles'; an example is the local council that wishes to cut down trees so that there is no risk of their falling on a ratepayer. Both the visual benefits of the trees and the possible effect on the health of a sufferer could properly be treated by the methods described.

Evaluation of health services

Public authorities are faced with a large number of choices which involve not only the fixing of an overall budget but also choices between such things as research and casualty treatment, prevention and cure, priorities between patients of different ages, different social classes, and so on.

Planning of educational services

Here the problem is not only of defining and quantifying the direct costs and effects of various educational measures but also the cumulative process started off by education in a community. Both these questions have received a most interesting theoretical treatment by J Lesourne in his book *Le Calcul Econo-mique*[15], but the present author has not so far come across any well-documented practical applications.

14

Private Decisions and the Public Interest

In this book I have attempted to describe a logical method for the presentation, discussion and decision of issues affecting the community as a whole. This chapter begins by summarizing the advantages and disadvantages of the method; it goes on to look at the problem of background data and then discusses the relationship between public and private decision.

ADVANTAGES AND LIMITATIONS

Advantages

Economic analysis is bedevilled by rules of thumb; in the area of commercial accounting these take the form of fixed attitudes about the depreciation of assets, the valuation of investments, the uses of 'marginal' costings, and so on. Similarly in the field of public decision, maxims are invented to the effect that transfer payments should be ignored, that a certain line of government action will produce inflation, that increased interest rates will attract higher levels of savings, and so on.

Many of these are based on experience over a relatively short period or in a relatively restricted set of circumstances. In order to examine their truth or the degree to which they can be applied to any practical problem it is essential that a sound theoretical framework should be available within which they can be discussed and to which the economist or other well-informed person can refer in order to clarify any doubts that they might have over the treatment of a certain item or over the exact point at which an assumption is introduced.

I have found the approach set out in this book extremely useful in this respect and hope that others will do so too. In particular, it seems to me to have the following fundamental advantages.

1   It sets out a comprehensive theory. By starting with the satisfaction of individuals and the importance the State attaches to them, one is able to arrive at usable expressions for the measurement of economic change without having to introduce a great deal of extraneous theory.

2   In the course of this derivation it is of course necessary to make a number of assumptions; these are, however, clearly identified, and, furthermore, one can see exactly to what extent they affect the analysis. In all cases it would be possible to continue the theoretical development even if the assumptions were to be abandoned; as the aim of these assumptions is to reduce problems to workable dimensions, however, it is obvious that any such relaxations will lead to a rather more lengthy result.

3   It forces people to state what their factual assumptions are. This is very much the main advantage of cost benefit techniques as applied in industry and is of great value both in improving decision processes and in making them more accessible to other interested parties.

4   It takes into account terms affecting people other than the body responsible for the decision; these are sometimes referred to an external-ities. Having defined the community from whose viewpoint the decision is being taken, it then goes on to identify the effects of a change on the members of that community.

    In some of the examples that have been discussed (the location of a factory or an investment in an underdeveloped country), these effects are economic; that is to say, they either appear in the 'books' of one of the enterprises in the economy or they involve individuals in expenditure for which they obtain no satisfaction. However, a framework is also provided for the treatment of so-called 'intangibles'; these are items such as pollution of leisure time, which up to now have often been simply ignored or else greatly exaggerated. These terms are expressed in the common unit of money and this makes it possible to carry out objective comparisons between economic and non-economic interests.

5   The process starts from the price system; in a competitive market this is an extremely effective permanent system of market research (or behavioural research), and methods of dealing with intangibles are also closely geared to 'revealed preference', that is, the behaviour of people and their expenditure in market or near market situations.

6   Because of the clarity of its layout, the form that we have adopted encourages discussion between economists. Because of confusion over assumptions concerning methods or facts, such discussion is not always as fruitful as it might be.

7   The end presentation ties in with procedures familiar to industrial analysts accustomed to calculations of the discounted cash flow type. There are, however, important differences between the interests of a company and those of the community and these are discussed in the last section of this chapter.

Limitations

No method is without its dangers; the fact that cost benefit analysis is an extremely satisfactory tool from many points of view should not lead one to overlook that its scope is essentially limited.

1   It is a method of quantification and therefore depends upon good underlying forecasts, a comprehensive identification of the effects of a choice and proper measurement of such things as intangibles. If any of these are lacking, the result may be positively misleading.

    It was noted in Chapter 1 that in a conflict between the views of an expert and the results of cost benefit analysis, it was most unwise to assume that the expert is wrong. In many cases it turns out that one of the factors has been wrongly interpreted or left out altogether. However, this is by no means an argument for relying solely on intuitive techniques. It indicates rather that those responsible for the analysis should maintain considerable flexibility and be willing to follow up any suggestion made by those operationally concerned. This is after all one of the fundamental rules of good management accountancy in an industrial context.

2   It does not replace a dynamic analysis of the system and its probable interactions with other systems. The starting point is essentially a set of forecasts of what will happen in each of the two alternatives of a given choice. It does not set out to indicate whether a certain set of economic decisions will lead to a stable or to an unstable result. For this, other tools such as simulation are fortunately available.

3   In some cases cost benefit analysis can be extremely expensive.

The cost

This requires closer study. It may be useful to distinguish between a number of different causes for the admittedly high cost of such operations as the Roskill Commission.

1   The cost of investigating aspects specific to the decision. This is an essential cost of any investigation. It may involve estimating capital expenditure at one or more different sites, the production of traffic forecasts in the case of a major transport investment, and so on. In almost all cases the expenditure involved is very much less than the potential loss if an uneconomic decision is taken. This potential loss should be estimated at the outset, however, and warning bells sounded as soon as the cost of the investigation starts to reach any substantial percentage of this total — say 1 per cent.

2   Investigations that involve questions of measurement that are not specific to the choice under consideration. These are in some sense investments and concern things like the evaluation of noise, time, educational states, and so on.

3   Computation. This covers the basic calculation and the production of sensitivity analysis; in the same way as for the investigation under paragraph 1, the cost is unlikely to be very great.

4   The cost of public discussion at hearings such as those of the Roskill Commission. In many cases the prime aim of such hearings is to make sure that everyone is able to present their case and to listen to the defence of arguments put forward by others. This is probably even more important that the influence of the process on the final decision. In a democracy it is most important that the different parties to a dispute in which emotion is likely to run high should be persuaded that the decision finally taken is the right one in the public interest. This inevitably involves considerable expense, as does democracy itself.

Given the existence of a reasonable data bank of agreed values for various intangibles and of a national plan giving background economic information, the analysis of most public investments should not be unduly costly. It is reduced to 1 and 4. Whether the further step of a public inquiry is desirable depends upon circumstances; however, in most cases I believe that it is, and that the inevitably high cost of such hearings cannot fairly be stated as a disadvantage of cost benefit analysis. Whatever the method of decision the problem of putting it over to the various interested parties is bound to be a difficult and fairly expensive one.

DATA FOR COST BENEFIT ANALYSIS

Data banks

In order that work should not be repeated and that the maximum use should be made of valid research, it is most important that 'data banks' should be set up containing the results of up-to-date analysis. For example, in the case of time, values are extremely specific to various pairs of uses of time, and it is important to be able to set up a grid of known points in order to be able to interpolate any specific problem that might not warrant original research.

A good example of such a collection of research findings is given by Harrison and Quarmby[7] in the paper on time that was referred to in Chapter 5, page 60.

It is equally most desirable that common units should be adopted. For example, in the case of noise, a wide variety of measurements are available; as far as possible international agreement should be reached on the most appropriate ones, so that research in one context can be used elsewhere.

One of the valuable functions of the recent Roskill Commission was to draw together such information as was available on the intangibles that were relevant to the Third London Airport; the main results of which have been noted in Chapters 4, 8 and 9 of this book.

Regional plans

In a number of the examples that have been examined, data was required about such things as the likely population of an area, the rate of growth of an economy, differential movements of certain prices, the likely pattern of unemployment, the importance placed by the Government on development in one region rather than in another, and so on. A great deal of unnecessary speculation and discussion can be avoided, as well as its associated costs, if a reasonably authoritative national plan is available.

It is interesting to notice that when a large group asks its subsidiary companies to set up a long-term plan, it is common to issue an economic brief; this gives background data of a general nature such as rates of inflation, growth of disposable income, and so on, so that all the estimates will be in some sense comparable. A national plan or set background of economic statistics can be useful in a similar way for public decisions. An example is the existence of a 10 per cent discount rate recommended by the British Treasury. If such national assumptions are not defined in advance, it is, however, often possible to make very important deductions from 'revealed preference' of Government decisions*.

Revealed preference of Government

In the discussion of weighting in Chapter 9, the argument that no weighting was required was based on the fact that the Government showed no sign of wishing to radically redistribute income. This is a far more convincing argument than any amount of theorizing on what the ideal social order might be; if any substantial body of opinion were in favour of a redistribution it would have had ample time to put forward its ideas; if politically acceptable, one of the two possible British

---

* Revealed preferences are usually discussed in terms of individuals; they refer to the possibility of deriving valuations for such things as time from the behaviour of individuals — their revealed preference — in situations in which they have to trade off time against money.

Governments would have had every opportunity by way of taxes, allowances, subsidies, and so on, to put the redistribution into force.

Such revealed preferences are, however, also applicable in a wide variety of other circumstances. For instance, a great deal of interesting information about the value of life and death, and the views of the Government on different states of health, should be obtainable by suitable analysis of past health service decisions.

Inevitably one of the interesting results of such an examination is to reveal past inconsistencies. However, when two decisions are apparently in conflict it is wise to examine them fairly closely to ensure that there is no factor which might not have been immediately apparent but which could have accounted for the difference. Taking the example of the factory location problem in Chapter 11, the decision to go to a new site would appear illogical to anyone who had not considered the existence of a security factor.

In the case of education, analysis of existing government decisions might well produce some interesting information which could serve as a basis for the discussion of subsequent decisions. The framework of cost benefit analysis is equally valuable in this analytical role, as it should enable us to isolate other measurable factors which might account for government action and then measure the intangible aspect the quantification of which has so far eluded us.

In the context of regional planning an interesting application is the preference expressed by the Government for the location of investments in one area rather than another; in the United Kingdom this is given by the development area provisions, and if one relied on these one would conclude that the country was divided into two priority categories and that the difference between the two amounted to some £5000 a job, that is, the average incidence of the grants given in the development areas.

THE COMPANY AND THE COMMUNITY

It has been noted that one of the advantages of the presentation used in this book is that it expressly mentions company profits; as defined, these account for the vast majority of the purely economic terms in many analyses. (By this we are referring to the fact that profits are defined to include all cash expenditure and receipts and that enterprises include not only traditional companies but also public authorities and central and local government, that is, all economic agents other than individuals.) However, there are a number of differences between the interests of an individual company and those of the community, and it seems very important that the industrial manager and the economist should be aware of these. It may be useful to think of the differences under two main classifications: the technical differences in the definition of the net profit position of an individual company and the outside effects of that company's action which are sometimes referred to as externalities; these latter items concern the effect on other economic agents and on intangibles.

Differences in definition of profit

Under the following conditions there will only be technical differences between the interests of a company and those of the community.

1 No change in consumption that brings no satisfaction.

2 No change in the use of outside resources.

3 Zero net effect of the decision on intangibles.

4 All other companies in a state of optimal management and only marginally affected by the decisions of the first company. By marginally is meant that their economic state does not change enough for them to experience any material change in profit.   In terms of the geometrical analogy on page 125 they do not move off the 'flat' top of their dome.

5 The methods of evaluation of 'profit' in the company's decision must be consistent with those used by the cost benefit analysis.

This section will discuss the situation that arises when the first four conditions are met; for a variety of reasons, which will now be examined, the last one is never completely true. Differences in interest caused by these slight dissimilarity of definitions have been referred to as 'technical differences'.

   Even if a company has carried out its evaluation using cash flow methods of the DCF type (that is, has used the total cash movements that have been described as profit, although the company may split them up into profit, investment and working capital), there will be three important differences of treatment; these concern tax (and perhaps other similar items such as rates), the treatment of prices and the interest rate used.

Tax

The example of factory location given in Chapter 11 showed that tax does not equally affect all items in a company's evaluation. In particular the acquisition of land is not allowable. Similarly stocks of raw materials are only a tax deduction once they enter into the production process and stocks of finished product may contain profits on which tax will be levied. Furthermore, in countries in which sales taxes are not recoverable by user companies, the latter will be discouraged from using items bearing such taxes whereas the Government would be happy for them to do so. This means that the action taken to optimize profits after tax will not optimize profit before tax.

   This situation may be summed up in Table 14.1, in which plus means that the community would be more favourable than the company to the item in question and zero denotes indifference.

	Community
Profit	0
Stockholding	+
Investments	+
Purchase tax items	+

Table 14.1

Note that companies will be more discouraged than the State by: (a) stockholding; (b) investment which cannot be written off immediately; and (c) consumption of goods which bear purchase tax.

In order to bring about identity of interest between the State and the company it would be necessary for the following measures to be taken.

(i)   Investments written off 100 per cent for tax purposes as they are acquired.

(ii) Allowance of purchases against profit as they are made and acceptance of zero stock valuation for finished product.

(iii) Remission of sales tax to companies purchasing items on ehich it is levied.

Constant prices

It was noted that the community carried out its evaluation of profits at constant prices. This is because the benefit to a company brought about by an increase in price is offset by an equal and opposite loss to the members of the community who receive no additional satisfaction from their additional expenditure. This produces differences in interest between the community and the company in pricing decisions which can be illustrated by Table 14.2. In this zero denotes that the decision is not in the interest of the party concerned and one indicates that it is.

	Price greater than marginal cost		Price less than marginal cost	
	Company	Country	Company	Country
Price decrease				
High elasticity	1	1	0	0
Low elasticity	0	1	0	0
Price increase				
High elasticity	0	0	1	1
Low elasticity	1	0	1	1

Table 14.2

From this table it can be seen that companies in a market in which elasticity for their product is low and whose existing prices are greater than marginal cost will tend to increase their prices (or decline to reduce them) although a reduction would be in the interests of the community. As conditions of low elasticity very often concern markets in which the consumer has no choice, for example, monopolies, this conclusion should not be particularly surprising.

Rates of interest

Enterprises very often use different rates of interest from those suggested by the community. Two special cases are as follows.

(a) Local authorities often use rates which are too low, for example, the 4 per cent suggested by the Treasury for use on housing projects. This will normally lead them to invest more than would appear to be in the public interest.

(b) Industrial companies generally use very much higher rates and this may force them to act against the community's interest, and perhaps even against their own, by investing too little. An example of this was a large international group which was concerned because so little was being invested in factory efficiency which, although low risk, often only gives mediocre yields.

　　One of the reasons why yields on, say, labour-saving plant are so low is that only a fraction of the total cost of the labour is borne by the company; this is partly the result of a government policy of subsidizing low income employees through council houses, family allowances, and so on. Whether these policies are justified or not on general social grounds they certainly lead to divergence of interest between the company and the community. They are a kind of purchase tax in reverse.

　　In the other direction companies might well be unduly hesitant to employ executives earning high salaries and paying large proportions of them in tax; these are effectively 'high purchase tax' items.

In most circumstances these differences are not very great. It is clearly in the community's interest to diminish them, as businesses are obviously going to continue to take their decisions in order to maximize their profits and it is highly desirable that this same aim should lead them also to maximize collective utility.

Other differences

The three main sources of 'externality' are as follows.

The effect of company decisions on the profits of other economic agents

The State as a tax collector has already been dealt with in the previous section. The example of an underdeveloped country showed that a similar situation arose when dealing with duty. This example also showed that in such a country local subcontracts could give rise to considerable profits by the subcontractors once these had been adjusted to take into account the low opportunity cost of labour.

Similarly in some countries governments have been tempted to force traffic to use nationalized railway systems, on the grounds that they possess large economies of scale and that the resource costs of carrying additional freight are very much lower than the price paid. An example of this was given by the Roskill Commission in which the siting of the Third London Airport would have considerable effects on the profits of the railway and also on those of a number of other enterprises.

The only way of avoiding such anomalies is for all enterprises to charge for their services at their marginal cost. Fortunately in most cases this is so – marginal cost includes the cost of capital; however, where it is not there are usually severe problems, particularly where marginal cost is well below average cost. Theoretically it could be in the community's interest for the Government to pay subsidies to such enterprises to ensure that they did not lose by marginal pricing and this would ensure that one source of discrepancy between a company's interests and those of the community was removed. However, the payment of such subsidies is often undesirable in practice for two reasons.

1   Subsidy payments, unless frequently reviewed, can lead to shocking economic inefficiency.

2   The economies of scale to which subsidies refer are quite often imaginary. In the discussion of the Roskill Commission we pointed out the existence of a widespread belief in such economies, and the fixed nature of indirect expenses, even where this bore no relation to reality.

Use of outside resources

In conditions of unemployment the community adds back the cost of labour to the profits of the enterprises concerned. The only way of placing a company in a similar position is for the State to give it some advantage, usually in the form of a tax rebate, which is conditional on the employment of a certain number of people. Taking the example of an underdeveloped country which was mentioned in Chapter 11, the government in question might share some of its advantage with the company in order to persuade it to invest; this sharing is generally in the form of pioneer tax relief or similar measures.

Intangibles and consumption without satisfaction

In a cost benefit analysis from the point of view of the community, full account is taken of effects of 'intangibles' on individuals, and also of consumption with no satisfaction.

In the case of a company, this is not always so and depends upon the provisions concerning compensation. Here we have a number of comments.

1   It is highly desirable that compensation arrangements should be intro-
    duced which reflect as nearly as possible the cost of various nuisances on
    the community. For example, companies, or individuals, creating noise
    should pay for it, and the payment should be directly linked to the
    noise created.
        Obviously no system will ever be perfect but the basic idea deserves
    wider acceptance than it is given in the present state of the law in most
    countries.

2   In most cases it is more economic to charge a realistic 'price' for a
    nuisance than to ban it altogether. For example, a tax on noise would
    probably be far more effective than an out-and-out ban, as such a ban
    would have to be fixed at a level that is now considered technically
    obtainable. A tax on total noise would provide a constant incentive for
    further reduction. Furthermore, the occasional case in which the cost
    of suppressing noise would be astronomical is allowed to continue with
    the person generating it paying the proper price.

3   It is common for time clauses to be included in industrial contracts; it
    would be interesting to see the results of similar provisions in, for
    example, the conditions governing travel; my attitude to a recent nine
    hour wait at an airport might have been altered considerably if I had been
    compensated for my trouble. Some move in this direction was made by
    the offer of free meals.

4   Similarly those who suffer from nuisances of various kinds should be
    compensated. Once again the principle is to a certain extent recognized
    in a very timid way by rating assessments. However, it was most
    disturbing to learn that even those in very high NNI contours would
    receive no compensation on the arrival of the Third London Airport.
    Other equally shocking cases have recently been given considerable
    publicity in connection with urban motorways.
        The introduction of proper schemes of compensation and taxation of
    this kind would have two very important advantages. First, they would
    greatly lessen opposition to legitimate projects; one very real and
    justifiable cause of the present outbursts of opposition on the announcing
    of almost any public investment scheme is the fact that people are not
    properly compensated. Second, it would mean that many problems that

might otherwise need cost benefit analysis would be solved by the enterprise responsible taking the factors into its own profit calculation automatically.

Conclusion

It is heartening that we have been able to suggest very simple ways in which the interests of a company can be made to coincide with the interests of the community as expressed by cost benefit analysis. At the hearings of the Roskill Commission it was somewhat disturbing to find that many of the witnesses regarded profit as a measure that had nothing to do with national interest and might indeed be in direct opposition to it. As profit is, and is likely to remain, the most frequently used tool of economic analysis such a conclusion would be very frightening.

Appendix 1

Technical Description of Cost Benefit Analysis

COLLECTIVE UTILITY

This appendix sets out the broad lines of the theoretical justification for the approach adopted in the body of Chapter 2. The starting point of the analysis is summed up in two points.

1   The satisfaction of an individual is linked to a variety of factors, many of which can be referred to as the consumption of goods and services. These latter are defined in a wide enough way to include time, amenity, noise, etc, and usually labour.

2   The common good or welfare of any group is determined by the satisfactions of its individual members — collective utility.

If q_i^k are the quantities q of goods and services i and the index k denotes people, these two statements can be written:

$$S_k = S_k(q_i^k)$$

(satisfaction is a function of consumption)

$$U = U\,(S_k)$$

(collective utility is a function of individual satisfactions.

CHANGE

Very small changes in the economy which affect only one period, for example, a year, will be looked at first. It is, of course, possible to cut up time in any way that is convenient; nevertheless, for our purposes, we generally find that the 12-months' period is the most useful. The change in collective utility is made up of the differences in individual satisfactions multiplied by the value placed by the community on each individual:

$$dU \;=\; \Sigma_k \,\frac{\partial U}{\partial S_k}\, dS_k$$

We can also write this:

$$dU \;=\; \Sigma_k \,U_k\, dS_k \qquad\qquad U_k \;=\; \frac{\partial U}{\partial S_k}$$

Prices must now be introduced. In most cases, it is reasonable to assume that there is a single price system for all individuals and that the latter maximize their satisfactions taking into account their revenue r_k and the prices p_i, that is:

$S_k\,(q\,_i^{\,k})$ is a maximum under the income constraint.

$$\Sigma_i p_i q_i^k \;=\; r_k$$

thus
$$S_{ki} \;=\; \frac{\partial S_k}{\partial r_k}\left(p_i + q_i\,\frac{\partial p_i}{\partial q_i^k}\right)$$

If it is further assumed that the unit price of any good is independent of the quantity consumed by an individual, one can write:

$$S_{ki} \;=\; \frac{\partial S_k}{\partial r_k}\, p_i \qquad\left(S_{ki} \;=\; \frac{\partial S_k}{\partial q_i}\right)$$

These assumptions are reasonable in the vast majority of cases. However, when this is not so, a correction factor can usually be introduced. An example is given on page 21.

This is simply to state in mathematical terms that the marginal increase in satisfaction derived from the consumption of an extra unit of good i is proportional to its cost. $\dfrac{\partial S_k}{\partial r_k}$ is the additional satisfaction that we give to individual k if we increase his income by one unit. The following can now be written:

$$dU = \Sigma_k U_k dS_k$$

$$= \Sigma_{ki} U_k S_{ki} dq_i^k$$

$$= \Sigma_{ki} U_k \frac{\partial S_k}{\partial r_k} p_i dq_i^k$$

This means that the change in collective utility is equal to the change in consumption of individuals, measured at the original price, multiplied by a weighting factor.

$$U_k \frac{\partial S_k}{\partial r_k}$$

However, some changes in consumption have no effect on satisfaction. An example is given when a new bypass enables savings in petrol for a given journey. Such goods will be denoted by q_i and other examples are given on page 25.

One of the most important theoretical assumptions must now be made. This concerns the optimal distribution of income. It can be stated as follows.

The state has no preference between giving a unit increase of income to one individual rather than to another. As U_k is the value to the community of a unit increase in satisfaction for k and $\frac{\partial S_k}{\partial r_k}$ is the increase in satisfaction of the individual k when he receives an additional unit of income, this assumption means that $U_k \frac{\partial S_k}{\partial r_k}$ is constant for all k. This constant can be made one by transforming the collective utility function. Thus comes the following basic result:

$$dU = \Sigma_{ki} p_i dq_i^k$$

This means that the change in collective utility in such a marginal movement in the economy is equal to the change in individual consumption evaluated at constant prices. (Excluding those items q_i which are forced on the consumer; we can call this consumption which brings no satisfaction.) It should be noted at this point that we do not need to take into account a term $\Sigma_k q_i^k dp_i$. This is because it has been possible to assume that no individual can affect prices.

BUSINESSES

The term that we have just derived is in fact not much use as it stands, because clearly we cannot measure all the individual consumptions. Therefore, it is often useful to transform part of the expression into terms relating to the profits of businesses. (In this connection, the definition of a business is a very wide one and refers to all economic agents other than individuals, for example, conventional companies, the state, and so on.) The following statement is now used, relating supply and demand.

$$\Sigma_k q_i^k = q_i = \Sigma_h q_{ih} + q_{io}$$

In this expression the q_{ih} are the quantities of i associated with business h: it states that the total consumption by individuals is equal to the total amounts associated with businesses making and using it, plus any external resources (say, imports). 'Economic goods' refers to those that enter into the accounts of some sort of business. In a change therefore:

$$p_i dq_i = \Sigma_h p_i dq_{ih} + p_i dq_{io}$$

for one product and

$$\Sigma_{ki} p_i dq_i^k + \Sigma_{ki} p_i dq_i^k = \Sigma_{hi} p_i dq_{ih} + \Sigma_i p_i dq_o$$

for all normal economic products and all individuals.

Notice that i here only covers consumer goods. However, all other transactions between companies clearly cancel out over the economy as a whole, and the only further change we need take into account is that concerning movements in the use of outside resources, for example, relating to unemployed labour. Now $\Sigma_{hi} p_i dq_{ih}$ is the profit of business h defined in cash terms, that is, excluding such notions as capitalization of fixed assets and depreciation, and is calculated at the price in force *before the change*. Thus:

Change in consumption of consumer goods by individuals	=	Change in profits of all businesses	+	Change in use of outside resources (imports, exports, etc) or under utilized resources (for example, unemployed labour)

Now, in the expression for the change in collective utility, there was the consumption of economic goods referred to above, plus movements in socio-economic ones such as time, less consumption of 'no-satisfaction' goods q_i. The following statement is then obtained.

In a marginal change, with the various assumptions we have indicated and notably a single price system and optimal distribution of income, the change in value to the community is as follows.

1   Change in profit of all companies evaluated at constant prices.

2   The change in consumption that brings no satisfaction.

3   Change in use of outside resources.

4   Change in consumption of socio-economic goods by individuals.

On page 11 we look at the case of two price systems corresponding to a difference in the cost of living.

The discussion on page 12 adds rather more details on consumption which does not affect the satisfaction of individuals. However, we are left with two important theoretical points.

(a)   When is a change marginal, and what is the effect on the theory if it is not?

(b)   How can we take into account more than one period?

MARGINAL/STRUCTURAL

The treatment of this case, which is common to many branches of science, is to consider the structural change as a series of marginal ones and to make assumptions similar to those put forward above for each of the steps. This has led to an expression for the change in collective utility:

$$U(2) -- U(1) = \int_1^2 \Sigma_i p_i \, dq_i$$

If the demand curve linking price and quantity consumed is a straight line, this expression can be simplified to:

$$\Sigma_i \frac{p_i(1) + p_i(0)}{2} (q_i(1) - q_i(0))$$

The difference here is that we would have to consider not only the change in volume looked at in our marginal section, but also a price effect. The decision whether a change is marginal or not depends not only upon the absolute sums involved but also upon the effect on the different economic agents. Thus, the changing of the site of a bridge might cost many millions of pounds but still have only a marginal effect on travellers or people living on both sides of the river.

TIME

Calculations such as the one just described can be carried out period by period giving a series of changes in collective utility. The question is now to bring these together into one figure. The solution depends upon the introduction of a notion of equivalence between periods from the point of view of the community. Once it is accepted that £1 today is worth more than £1 tomorrow an assumption that is clearly borne out by public investment programmes, one can write:

$$V(1) = (1 + p) V(0)$$

Where $V(1)$ is the value of £1 at the end of 1 year and $V(0)$ the value at the beginning of the year. This leads to the normal relationship for dealing with the discounting of cash flows:

$$V(r) = (1 + p)^r V(0)$$

$$\text{or } V(0) = \frac{V(r)}{(1 + p)^r}$$

Where $V(r)$ is the value of £1 after r years.

TWO PRICE LEVELS

Consider a situation in which two towns have different price levels p_i (1) and p_i (2). Suppose an individual moves from one to the other. His satisfaction will change as the income constraint will force a movement in his total consumption of:

$$\Sigma_i q_i^k (p_i(1) - p_i(2))$$

(One of the q_i may well be labour and this does not therefore imply that his income is constant.)

In order to restore him (and the collective utility to his previous level, one would have to give him an additional income of:

$$\Sigma_i q_i^k (p_i(2) - p_i(1))$$

This means that in the term for the change in collective utility, a correction should be added expressing the change in the cost of living evaluated at the original levels of consumption of individuals who move multiplied by the difference between the two levels of prices before the change.

A similar term can be introduced relating to socio-economic goods. If an individual is obliged to move to a more noisy area, all things being equal, the country suffers a loss because of his reduction in satisfaction. This needs to be deducted when calculating the overall effect of the change.

CONSUMPTION THAT DOES NOT AFFECT SATISFACTION

The following is the case of a new road that allows an individual to save consumption of petrol for his private car.

Assuming that the total traffic on the route stays constant the fact of saving petrol will not affect anyone's satisfaction directly. This introduces a 'bonus' into the system equivalent to the saving in petrol; this is of course spent on other goods which confer satisfaction equivalent to the value of the petrol saved. However, the point here is that contrary to the normal situation, this is not offset by a similar loss corresponding to a reduction in consumption. This arises because the service consumed is a journey and not a gallon of petrol.

Another way of looking at this would be to separate the role of an individual as a consumer from that as a transporter in his own private car. As the journey is unaffected, he has no change in satisfaction. However, his car business makes a profit equivalent to the saving in petrol and this will appear in the collective utility.

A similar case arises when looking at removal expenses forced on a consumer by, for example, slum clearance. If the employer recognizes this cost, a corresponding term will appear in the collective utility as a loss of profit. However, if not, we must introduce a correction factor. Of course this case does not apply to moves which are made by individuals for their own satisfaction, to live in a more attractive neighbourhood, for example. Here the expense is part of the cost of an improved housing service.

Appendix 2

Condorcet's Paradox

The phenomenon described as Condorcet's paradox illustrates the fact that groups of individuals are not always transitive in their choices; this means that if they prefer A to B and B to C they do not necessarily prefer A to C. The following example is based on a group of individuals who have to make a series of comparisons between three possible choices of a meeting place and is supposed to be based on that august institution, the Academie Française. The forty members have split up into six groups corresponding to the six possible ways of ranking the three alternative meeting places, the Institut, the Sorbonne and Versailles. The last three columns show the votes that would be obtained for the following propositions.

Move from the Institut to Versailles
Move from Versailles to the Sorbonne
Move from the Sorbonne to the Institut

Group	Preference 1	2	3	Number	V	S	I
A	I	S	V	11	—	11	11
B	S	V	I	9	9	9	—
C	V	I	S	6	6	—	6
D	V	S	I	7	7	—	—
E	I	V	S	4	—	—	4
F	S	I	V	3	—	3	—
				40	22	23	21

189

It should be noticed that there is no question of individuals changing their preferences during the experiment; they remain consistent throughout. The point is that the group prefers Versailles to the Institut and the Sorbonne to Versailles but does not prefer the Sorbonne to the Institut. In other words they are not transitive. If such a body were to base decisions on a majority vote, they would circulate indefinitely between the three sites.

It should be noted that this has nothing to do with the people concerned becoming tired of a site and wanting a change; no information is added during the process and the instability of the situation is an independent phenomenon.

Appendix 3

Value of Land

THE PROBLEM

In the UK, there is a very large difference between the economic value of land as an agricultural resource (perhaps £50 an acre), its market price (say £500 an acre) and its value for development (say £30 000 an acre). In many planning studies, the choice of an appropriate value could be critical. A site of 1000 acres would be valued at anything between £50 000 and £30m.

THE TEXTBOOK ANSWER

In terms of the general theory set out in this book, we would normally credit any solution which released land with its value for development. The justification for taking this value as a benefit is that someone would pay a given amount for a house built on that land; this amount would include the value of the land and there is no reason to suppose that the satisfaction obtained by the individual is less than the price that he is prepared to pay.

The question would then be raised as to whether the availability of this land would produce changes elsewhere in the economy, and in particular whether these would go some way to offsetting this benefit. Here there appear to be two extreme possibilities covering what would happen if this land had not been made available.

1   New houses would be built on less land per house; this would imply that the value of the land to the house purchaser was approximately equal to its market price (strictly speaking, this assumes that the changes involved are marginal).

2   More land is taken from alternative uses, that is, agriculture. If this is so we should credit our project with the sum of the following.

    (a)   The economic value of the agriculture which can now continue.

    (b)   An estimate of the locational advantage of the site we are valuing compared to that agricultural land. This estimate also includes the value of any infrastructure at the site that would otherwise be unused.

    (c)   The amenity value of the agricultural land.

In principle, the market price should be equal to the aforementioned three terms; a face value interpretation of Government policy on planning would indicate that they had no preference as between liberating the land for development and thus procuring a benefit equal to the market price, and removing an equivalent amount of land from agriculture, imposing locational disadvantages and abandoning a piece of planning control. If this were true, it would mean that the two alternatives mentioned are equivalent, and that we should use the market price. We will examine a number of objections to this in the following paragraph; however, it should be pointed out that any abandonement of the market price is a serious matter and that it would have serious repercussions on decision-taking over a wide range of topics.

OBJECTIONS TO MARKET PRICE

It seems appropriate to consider three objections to the conclusions of the previous paragraph.

1   The equivalence stated in the preceding paragraph is not really a reflection of Government policy.

2   Prices applicable for relatively small parcels of land are not appropriate to the relatively large areas used for public sector development (the penny packets argument).

3   The price of land is unreal in that few people actually pay it.

Government policy

We have stated that the market price of development land must be equal to its agricultural value plus its locational advantages plus a value placed on the mainten-ance of planning restrictions. It could be argued that this is wholly theoretical and that the very substantial premium relating to planning is wholly artificial. This is a dangerous argument and one which we consider inappropriate. For many years, Governments have been aware of the price burden resulting from planning restrictions and are apparently willing to see the community bear it.

Penny packets

The areas of land involved can vary very considerably in size; however, in choosing a value, we should look for one which has been based on areas of similar size. In particular such a value must take into account the availability of services, roads and so on. It would not be appropriate to base the price on a 1-acre plot having access to an otherwise fully developed road.

Do people pay the price?

There is little doubt that the value of land is inflated due to a number of reasons of which two seem particularly important.

(a) The joint effect of inflation, interest rates and tax relief. This may be illustrated by the case of an individual who actually makes money by borrowing under current conditions for house purchase. By this, we mean that the decrease in his real debt is greater than the net interest paid in any year. Similar considerations apply to industrial purchases.

(b) Other tax considerations relating to land, for example, estate duty, pro-visions.

These objections seem to be far more fundamental than either of the previous two. Our justification for including the market price of land was basically that indi-viduals were prepared to pay it at the margin and, therefore, were getting satis-faction proportionately to that price. However, if it turns out that most individuals buying land are in fact paying nothing for it, then this would indicate a very sharply reduced valuation.

CONCLUSION

It is almost certain that the market price of land is too high to be taken into account in cost benefit evaluations. This is basically because no one effectively pays this market price. Further research on this problem would undoubtedly be rewarding; this might include an analysis of the extent to which the final con-sumer actually pays for land in any real sense.

References

0   Arrow, Kenneth J., *Social Choice and Individual Values.* Cowles Foundation for Research in Economics at Yale University, New York; Wiley (1970).

1   Papers and Proceedings of the Committee on the Third London Airport, Chairman: the Rt. Hon. Eustice Roskill, Vol VII, HMSO, London, 1969.

2   Boulanger, H. Hubert le and Roy, Bernard, L'Enterprise facé a la selection et a l'orientation des projets de recherche: la methodologie en usage dans le group SEMA (B); VII, *Metra*, 1968.

3   Witt, F. de., 'La France de l'an 2000', *Expansion*, June 1970.

4   Kendall, P.M.H., Rijnmond Public Authority — Industrial location project. Metra Consulting Group, London, 1970 — 1973.

5   Civil Aviation Act, 1949, Part Act Ch. 67, Session 12 and 13 of G VI, HMSO, London.

6   Becker, G.S., 'A theory of the allocation of time', *Economic J.,* 493, 1965.

7   Harrison, A.J. and Quarmby, D.A., 'Value of time in transport planning: a review', European Conference of Ministers of Transport (ECMT), Paris, 1969.

8   Thomas, Thomas C., 'The value of time for passenger cars an experimental study of commuter values', Stanford Research Institute, Palo Alto, 1967.

9   Final Report on the Problem of Noise, Chairman: Sir Alan Wilson, FRS, March Cmnd 2056, HMSO, London, 1963.

10   Kryter, K.D., 'Scaling human reactions to the sound from aircraft', *J. Acoust. Soc. AM.,* 31, 1415, 1959.

11   Sibert, E., 'Aircraft Noise and development control: the policy for Gatwick Airport', *J. Town Planning Institute,* 55, No 4, 149, 1969.

12   Plowden, S., 'Environment and planning: evidence to the commission on the third London airport', 196, stage 5, Subject Group F.

13 'Pourrez vous baigner cette été', *Que Choisir,* No 42, 839, 1970.

14 Foster, C.D. and Beasley, M.E., Estimating the social benefit of constructing an underground railway in London, *J Roy. Stat. Soc.,* Ser.A., 126, 46, 1963.

15 Lesourne, J., *Le Calcul Economique,* Dunod, Paris, 1964. English speaking edition *Cost Benefit Analysis and Economic Theory,* North Holland Press, Amsterdam, (1975).

16 Statement to the Commons by Mr Anthony Crosland, May 1968, *Hansard* 765, 32, HMSO, London.

17 'The Channel Tunnel: economic and financial studies', a Report prepared by Coopers and Lybrand Associates Ltd., and SETEC — Economie, Paris, for the British Channel Tunnel Company Ltd. and the Societé Française du Tunnel sous la Manche.

18 Department of the Environment, 'The Channel Tunnel Project', Cmnd 5256, HMSO, London, 1973.

19 Generalised costs and estimation of movement cost and benefits in transport planning, Department of the Environment Mathematical Advisory Unit, Note 179.

20 Young, M. and Willmott, P., *Family and Kinship in the East End of London,* Pelican, London, 1962.

Index